HOW TO DO
just about
ANYTHING IN
Microsoft®
Windows®XP

Reader's Digest

HOW TO DO just about ANYTHING IN

Microsoft®
Windows®XP

Published by The Reader's Digest Association Limited
London • New York • Sydney • Montreal

How to do just about anything in Microsoft® Windows® XP

was edited and designed by The Reader's Digest Association Limited, London

First edition Copyright ©2003
The Reader's Digest Association Limited,
11 Westferry Circus, Canary Wharf, London E14 4HE.
www.readersdigest.co.uk

Reprinted 2005

We are committed to both the quality of our products and the service we provide to our customers.
We value your comments, so please feel free to contact us on **08705 113366**, or via our Web site at
www.readersdigest.co.uk
If you have any comments or suggestions about this book, e-mail us at: **gbeditorial@readersdigest.co.uk**

Printing and binding: Hung Hing Off-Set Printing Co. Ltd., Hong Kong

Contents

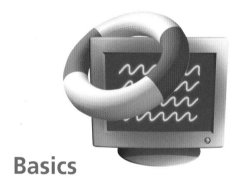

Basics

Customising Windows

Windows' Built-in Programs

Good Housekeeping

Troubleshooting

How to use this book

This book makes learning to use Windows both easy and enjoyable. Each task is set out clearly and is accompanied by pictures that show you what you will see on your screen. You'll never be left wondering where to find a command or how to complete a task. And the book includes a wealth of expert advice, tips and inspirational ideas to help you make the most of Windows.

GETTING AROUND THE BOOK
The five sections in this book take you through setting up your PC, mastering Windows activities and keeping your computer in good working order.

Basics
In this introductory section on using Windows XP, you'll find out how Windows works and how to get around your system quickly and easily. You'll also learn how to save and delete files, and pick up handy tips on organising your work.

Customising Windows
Windows comes with standard settings, but you can adapt these to suit your needs. You can change your Desktop background, create shortcuts to programs and folders you use often, and customise controls to make them more convenient for you to use.

Windows' Built-in Programs
Before you rush out and buy expensive software, try out the programs that come ready installed with Windows. These include simple word processors, a basic graphics program and a range of multimedia options for playing CDs or editing movies.

Good Housekeeping
Over time, your PC's hard disk can get filled up with redundant documents and programs. And glitches and viruses can make your computer crash or work much slower than before. Most mishaps are easily solved once you know how. Find out how to maintain your hard disk at its optimum capability.

Troubleshooting
Your PC and its software can behave unexpectedly. If this happens to you, there's no need to panic. This section covers common problems and offers easy-to-follow solutions.

WHICH SOFTWARE?
This book assumes that you're using a PC with Windows XP Home edition. The snapshots of a PC screen are of Windows XP as it looks after a brand new installation, but four main Desktop icons have been added (see page 12). If the windows and folders look slightly different from those on your screen, don't worry; all the features and tools are exactly the same.

Close up
These project-related tips give further insight into how Windows works.

Bright idea
Make the most of Windows with these inspiring suggestions.

Key word
You'll find handy definitions of technical words or phrases here.

GETTING AROUND THE PAGE

You are guided through the tasks in this book by means of illustrated steps and a range of visual features. Here are the key items you should look for on each page.

Before you start
Step-by-step projects begin with a section of text with points to consider, programs to open and tasks to do before beginning the project.

Snapshots
Pictures of the PC screen – 'snapshots' – show you what you should see on your monitor at the point they appear in the project. Often more than one snapshot is shown in a step.

Step-by-step
Projects and tasks are set out in easy-to-follow steps, from the first mouse click to the last. You are told which keyboard and mouse commands to issue, and the programs, folders and menus you need to access.

Magnifications
Snapshots of the PC screen that require special attention are magnified so that you can see them more clearly.

Type in quotes
Quotation marks indicate either the exact words you'll see on your screen, or what you need to type in as part of a step.

Bold type
Any bold text is a command for you to carry out. You might need to select a menu option, a toolbar button, a dialogue box tab, or press a key.

Useful tips
Near the main block of text are explanations of the more complex aspects of a task and alternative ways to do things.

Page turns
The orange arrow indicates that your project continues over the page.

Features
Sometimes a topic is presented as a feature, giving lots of general advice and tips, rather than explaining a specific task in a step-by-step format. Often, annotated images will illustrate items of particular importance.

Maximise your disk space

As you create more and more files and install new programs on your PC, your hard disk will start to fill up. If your hard disk gets too full, you will run out of room to install further programs and your PC may slow down. Keep an eye on how much space you have and regularly delete old folders and files to help keep your PC running smoothly.

Quick keyboard commands

Nearly all the actions or commands you perform with your mouse can also be done by pressing 'hot keys' – these are single keys or combinations of keys. For example, you can access the Start menu by pressing the 'Windows' key at the bottom left of your keyboard, or you can open My Computer by pressing the 'Windows' and 'E' keys together.

That's amazing!
Items of special interest, and inspiring ideas and explanations, which you can use to enhance the way you work with Windows XP.

Watch out
These tips warn you of potential difficulties and pitfalls when using Windows XP, and give helpful advice on how to avoid problems.

Expert advice
Advanced guidance and smart tips on specific features, and advice on how to get professional results with Windows XP.

Set up your PC safely

When you are choosing a suitable location for your PC, check that there is enough space for all the equipment and an adequate number of mains outlets. You also need to consider lighting and seating, and the surface area of your desk. If you want to connect to the Internet or send faxes from your computer, you will also need to be near a telephone socket.

SITTING AT YOUR COMPUTER

You need to think carefully about how to arrange your work area, as a poorly laid out computer desk and PC will be tiring to use and may prevent you from operating your PC properly.

If you find yourself leaning towards the monitor, increase the zoom level at which you are viewing your document.

Your legs should remain uncrossed and your knees should be lower than your hips.

An adjustable chair will support your back and can be altered to suit each family user.

The monitor should be around 50cm from your eyes.

Your desk should be a comfortable height for typing, with your upper arms parallel to your body and your lower arms parallel to the floor.

Your feet should rest flat on the floor.

NAMING AND PLACING PARTS

Your PC's hardware includes all the parts that you can actually see and handle. Knowing how to position these elements ensures a safe and efficient work area.

System unit
This is the part of your computer to which everything is connected. Leave space so that you can plug in the cables easily and to allow for ventilation. Don't leave cables trailing.

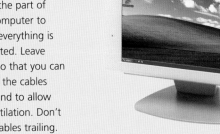

Monitor
This is the computer's screen. Position your monitor to avoid reflections, but do not face a bright window yourself as this may lead to eyestrain.

Speakers
For the best sound quality, speakers should be well spaced apart on either side of the monitor and at desk level or higher, not just pushed under the desk.

Printer
Position your printer near the system unit. Make sure there is sufficient space around it for loading the paper trays.

Keyboard
Make sure the keyboard is on a stable and level surface within easy reach. Leave enough space in front of it for hands and wrists. Ensure that the desk is at the correct height.

Mouse
Place the mouse to the side of your keyboard that suits whether you are left- or right-handed. Use a mouse mat to create the correct amount of friction, and be sure there is plenty of room to move the mouse around.

Expert advice
If you are planning to use your computer for long periods, either surfing the Internet or preparing your accounts and letters, then you should invest in a good-quality comfortable office chair. Most dining chairs do not offer the support for your back that is vitally important when you are sitting still for long periods. Also, most office chairs are adjustable and so will suit every member of the family. Remember, even with a comfortable chair, you should take regular 10 minute breaks to walk around.

What is Windows?

Your computer uses a piece of software called an 'operating system' in order to run programs and control its hardware. The system used on most PCs is Windows. It provides the connection between the user and the software, and allows the PC to perform tasks, such as printing. Windows XP, the most recent version of Windows, is fast, reliable, and very easy to use.

SEE ALSO...
- *What you see first* p 18
- *Moving around a window* p 20
- *Change your settings* p 42

WINDOWS

Using Windows is not as difficult as it may seem. The general principles of working with an operating system are easy to learn, and you'll be surprised at how often the same processes crop up, even in different programs. In fact, Windows is designed this way – if you know how to open and save a file in one program, you will be able to do it in all Windows-compatible programs.

Operating system

The term 'operating system' refers to software that enables the computer's hardware to 'talk' to its programs and its users. While people communicate with words, the computer uses a digital language of electrical 'on' and 'off' pulses. The operating system translates your key presses, mouse movements and clicks into a binary language of 1s (on) and 0s (off), which the PC's processor can understand and manipulate. Once the task is finished, the results are translated back into a form we can read on the screen.

Quick Desktop tour

If you bought a computer with Windows XP pre-installed, you may only be able to see the Recycle Bin on your Desktop. However, you can add icons for quick access to other areas of your PC, the Internet and any other computers linked to yours. To do this, right-click on a blank area of the Desktop and choose **Properties**. Select the **Desktop** tab, click on the **Customize Desktop** button and put ticks next to 'My Documents', 'My Network Places', 'My Computer' and 'Internet Explorer'. Then click on **OK** and on **OK** again. Icons can represent physical components, such as your hard disk or a printer, or virtual locations on your hard disk, such as the Recycle Bin or the My Documents folder. When you install a new program, a shortcut icon may appear on your Desktop, usually with a small black arrow in the corner. To access the program, place the mouse pointer over the icon and double-click.

Start menu

The Start menu contains shortcuts to your PC's software. Click on the **Start** button, then on **All Programs** and you'll see a list of applications.

Just click on one, and the program opens. The Start menu enables you to quickly access recently used documents and the programs you use most often. From here, you can also adjust your PC's settings, search for files, browse the Internet and look for help on a variety of topics.

Dialogue boxes

Sometimes Windows and its programs need instructions. When this happens, you use an on-screen dialogue box to make choices – the box may pop up and ask you to confirm or alter an action or it may appear after you click on a menu item or button, offering a range of options to tick or select. One of the most common dialogue boxes appears when you close a file. If you haven't saved since you last made changes to that file, the dialogue box will give you the option to save it before closing.

Key word

A program is software designed to allow the user to carry out a specific task, such as writing a letter or calculating a bank balance. To see which programs are on your PC, click on the Start button and then on All Programs.

THE WORLD OF WINDOWS

Every program or file you open is viewed on screen in a 'window' on the surrounding Desktop. Your Desktop may look slightly different from the one shown here, depending on whether you upgraded to XP or bought a PC with it pre-installed.

My Documents Double-clicking on this icon opens the My Documents window.

My Computer window Easy access to files and folders in the various drives on your PC.

Title bar Dark when active, light when inactive, it shows the window's name and icon.

Minimize, Maximize and Restore Minimize (left) reduces a window to a button on the Taskbar. Maximize (right) expands a window to fill the Desktop; click on this button again to restore a window to its original size.

User name Displays the user who is currently logged onto your PC.

Frequently used programs The six programs you use most often are listed here.

Control Panel Allows you to change your computer's settings.

All Programs Gives you access to all the programs on your PC.

Start button Click here and navigate pop-up menus to access most items on your PC.

Close Shuts a window or program.

Menu bar Lists the series of drop-down menus containing commands.

Standard Buttons Toolbar Offers access to frequently used commands and tools.

Address bar Shows where you are and gives you access to other drives on your PC and Web locations.

Recycle Bin This is where your deleted files are stored, ready for final removal.

Quick Launch An area where you can put shortcuts to favourite programs.

Program and window buttons The active program button is dark blue. Other programs and minimised windows are light blue. Click once to select an item.

Taskbar Contains the **Start** button and useful shortcuts.

Notification area Change date and time, and set the volume level here.

Expert advice
If you can't see the Quick Launch Toolbar, right-click on the **Taskbar** and select **Toolbars** followed by **Quick Launch**. A row of icons will appear just to the right of the Start button (see above). You can add your own shortcuts to this area by clicking and dragging. If there isn't room for new icons, right-click on the **Taskbar** and click on **Lock the Taskbar** to remove the tick. Then drag the vertical dotted line to the right. Finally, right-click on the **Taskbar** and select **Lock the Taskbar** again.

Close up
When you double-click on a document to open it, the program in which it was created should open automatically. This means you do not need to open the program separately before you can access the document.

THE WORLD OF WINDOWS

The Windows operating system has been updated many times since it was introduced in 1983. It is now capable of performing a wide array of tasks.

A brief history

The original Microsoft operating system was called MS-DOS (Microsoft – Disk Operating System). To instruct the computer to carry out an action, you typed your commands into a text-only screen. It was successful and reliable but not particularly easy to use, as you had to learn complex instructions for individual actions.

Windows 3.1, released in 1992, used a 'GUI' (Graphical User Interface), which featured simple screen icons and windows. You could point, click on and drag and drop icons with a mouse to give your PC instructions.

The next major upgrades to the system were Windows 95, Windows 98 and Window Me. The most recent version is Windows XP. This combines the multimedia features of Windows Me with the reliability and speed of the Windows 2000 operating system, which was developed primarily for business users.

Keep up to date

The Microsoft Corporation work continually on their software to fix problems, or 'bugs', which arise with new versions, and to improve Windows' performance. You can download the latest updates to your current operating system free of charge from the Internet. Just click on

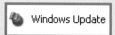

the **Start** button and select **All programs**, followed by **Windows Update**. This starts your Internet browser program and, once you're connected to the Internet, accesses Microsoft's Web site for information and downloads.

Help and Support

Windows has a useful Help system as well as Troubleshooting features to answer questions, guide you through tasks and help you to solve problems (see page 85). The Help menu, on the right of the Menu bar, offers options relevant to the current program. Help may also appear as a small '?' button on the far right of a window's Title bar. If you click on this, a '?' symbol appears, which stays with the mouse pointer. When you click on an item or command on which you need help, an information box will be displayed.

To open the 'Help and Support Center', click on the **Start** button and select **Help and Support** from the pop-up menu. This displays help categories and topics, and provides links to the Web for further help. Certain tasks have

'wizards' associated with them, which offer step-by-step instructions in dialogue boxes to guide you through the specific task. Troubleshooting Wizards diagnose and solve technical problems, and can be accessed via Help and Support.

Programs galore

Your PC comes with a variety of programs already installed. There is a basic text editing program called Notepad and a word processor called WordPad. There is also an Address Book, a Calculator, a graphics package called Paint and, under Accessories, a music and video centre

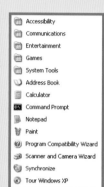

called Windows Media Player. The Media Player can be used to play CDs and **MP3** files. It will also play most video formats, and you can even listen to your favourite radio station through your computer's speakers using Media Player's Internet Radio Station Finder.

Windows Movie Maker is also included, which enables you to import, edit and save your home movies on your computer. And transferring digital images onto your computer's hard disk is easier than ever now that Windows XP helps you copy your pictures from a digital camera or a scanner.

Key word

***MP3** is short for 'MPEG audio Layer-3' and is a technology and format for compressing audio files. MP3 files are much smaller than the original audio files, yet the sound quality remains high. These smaller files are ideal for use on portable music players and on the Internet.*

Watch out

Make sure you buy the correct version of Windows XP. There is an upgrade from Windows 98 or Windows Me or a full version for people who can't upgrade, for example, those with Windows 95. It is easy to upgrade or install – just put the CD-ROM in your disc drive, and the setup software will do everything else for you. If you are upgrading, you will need your previous WIndows CD-ROM.

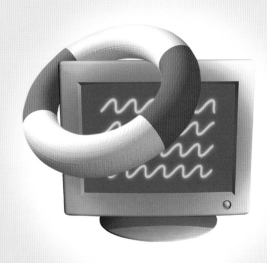

Basics

You and your computer

A PC is made up of interconnected physical components called 'hardware'. The programs that allow it to perform specific tasks are called 'software'. The operating system is a program that enables the hardware and software to talk to each other and to communicate with the user. It then carries out the commands and displays the results on the monitor.

SEE ALSO...
- *Set up your PC safely p 10*
- *What you see first p 18*

YOUR COMPUTER
It can be useful to understand how your PC's parts interact.

What's in the box?
Your computer hardware includes:
- RAM (Random Access Memory), which stores information about open documents and programs while the PC is switched on.
- A processor, or 'chip', which acts as the PC's brain, carrying out calculations and operations.
- A hard disk, which stores the operating system, program files and documents that you have created, even when the power is off.
- CD or DVD-ROM drive.
- Floppy disk drive.
- Ports, such as the PS/2 and USB connectors, and adaptors, such as your sound card, which provide the connections between hardware and software.

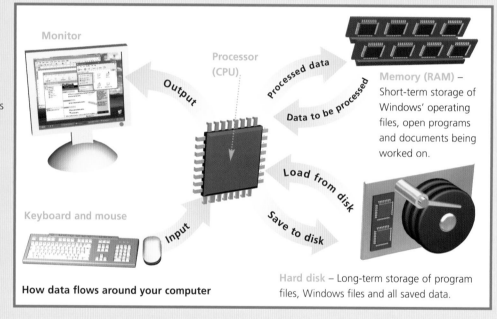

Monitor

Processor (CPU)

Output

Processed data

Data to be processed

Memory (RAM) – Short-term storage of Windows' operating files, open programs and documents being worked on.

Load from disk

Save to disk

Keyboard and mouse

Input

How data flows around your computer

Hard disk – Long-term storage of program files, Windows files and all saved data.

Bright idea
Remember to save your work regularly in case there is a power failure or your computer crashes. This is because RAM is only a temporary form of memory and the data it stores is lost when there is no power supplied to your PC.

The hard disk

This device is the computer's permanent internal storage area. It is made up of double-sided thin circular 'platters' and moving read/write heads. The hard disk stores all data, such as the Windows operating system files, application data, saved documents, your settings and even the way Windows looks on your Desktop. Every time you install a program, alter a program's or Windows' settings, or save a file, some data on the hard disk is rewritten.

RAM

Random Access Memory (RAM) is your PC's memory – a temporary electronic storage space for digital data while your PC is switched on. Data stored in RAM can be accessed much more quickly than if it was on the hard disk, and this allows your PC to work faster. The Windows XP recommended requirement for RAM is 128MB. However, 256MB or 512MB will make your PC run more quickly.

Units of data storage

The smallest amount of information that can be stored on a hard disk or in RAM is a 'bit' (short for **b**inary dig**it**). Eight bits make up a 'byte' (**b**inary **te**rm), which is enough space to store a letter or a number. You may hear 'Kilobyte' (KB) used as a measure of storage. This equals 1024 bytes. Note that Kilobit (Kb) is used for data rates, for example in describing modem speeds. A 'Megabyte' (MB) is equal to 1024 Kilobytes, and a 'Gigabyte' (GB) equals 1024 Megabytes.

The processor

Sometimes called a microprocessor or CPU (Central Processing Unit), this is the brains of the PC. It carries out the calculations that allow the computer to work. The processor performs millions of calculations every second. Processor speed is measured in hertz (Hz). A 3GHz (gigahertz) processor works faster than one with a speed of 900MHz (megahertz).

Motherboard

All hardware is housed on, or connected to, the motherboard, which is your PC's main circuit board. External hardware, such as your printer and monitor, is connected to it via cables. The mouse and keyboard can be connected by cables or by a wireless connection.

The mouse

Desktop PCs come with a mouse as one of the main 'input devices' (laptops usually have a rectangular 'touch pad'). When you move the mouse, the mouse pointer on the screen moves in the same relative direction – you use it to point to and select objects on screen, to open folders and documents, and to issue commands by clicking on-screen buttons.

A basic mouse has two buttons – the left one is used the most. A single click of the left mouse button on an icon, file or folder will select or highlight it. Any of these items can be activated or opened by a double-click (two quick clicks without moving the mouse). A single click on a button, a link on a Web

site, or a menu item will activate it. Clicking some items once with the right mouse button (it never needs to be double-clicked) activates a pop-up menu giving access to shortcuts and extra functions relating to that item. If your mouse is quite new, it may have a small wheel between the two buttons. By rolling this wheel forward or backward you can scroll down or across a window rather than using the scroll bars. You can usually customise the mouse wheel to perform an action, such as a double-click, when it is pressed.

The keyboard

Apart from using the keyboard to type in text, you can also use it to do almost everything the mouse does. You can scroll through windows using the up and down arrows and there are many 'hot keys' that are shortcuts to menu or toolbar commands.

Watch out

Floppy disks and portable storage media, such as Zip disks, are written magnetically. Do not store them near magnets or stereo speakers, which have large electromagnets inside, otherwise you risk corrupting the information on the disks.

Close up

If your mouse is at the edge of the mat but the cursor isn't where you want it to be on the screen, lift the mouse up to move it to the middle of the mat. The cursor only moves when the ball under the mouse is rolling on a surface.

What you see first

Every Windows operation takes place on the 'Desktop'. This is a virtual workspace from which you can access all the programs and files on your PC. You can choose what to place on the Desktop, either filling it with shortcut icons to your frequently used programs and folders, or leaving it free of clutter as a colourful backdrop to your work.

SEE ALSO...
- *Using the Start menu* p 22
- *Personalise your Desktop* p 40
- *Create your own shortcuts* p 48

THE DESKTOP WINDOW

There are three main areas on the Desktop: the Taskbar (and its elements); the Desktop area or 'background'; and the Desktop icons.

Taskbar

Running along the bottom of the Desktop screen, the Taskbar contains the Start button and Quick Launch Toolbar (see page 13) on the left, and the 'notification area' on the far right. As you open new windows, they will appear as buttons on the Taskbar. You can reduce, or 'minimise', a window on the Desktop to a button on the Taskbar so that you can see other

 items. To do this, simply click on the – button (left) near the top right-hand corner of a window. To view the window again, click on its associated button on the Taskbar and it will be restored.

Start button

 Located on the left of the Taskbar, this button opens a menu, which gives access to programs and other facilities on your PC.

Quick Launch Toolbar

This toolbar allows you to 'launch' programs with a single mouse click but it may be hidden, depending on how Windows is set up. If it is not displayed, follow the instructions on page 13 to view it. You can drag icons here to make shortcuts. The default ones are, from left

 to right: Internet Explorer, which is a Web browser; Show Desktop, which minimises all open windows to the Taskbar; and Windows Media Player, which lets you play digital music and video files from a variety of sources.

Notification area

This holds a variety of useful icons, depending on what software and utilities are installed. The permanent ones are Volume Control and the Clock. Any extra items not in use are hidden, but can be viewed by clicking on an arrow button. To the left of the notification area is the Language Bar button ('EN' below). This allows you to control input language and speech recognition.

Close up
You can have the Taskbar hide itself automatically when you don't need it. Right-click on the Taskbar *and choose* Properties*. Then put a tick next to 'Auto-hide the taskbar' and click on* OK*. Now to see the Taskbar, just move your mouse pointer down to the bottom of the screen and it will pop up.*

YOUR DESKTOP

If you have a new PC or have installed Windows XP from scratch, you may only be able to see the Recycle Bin icon. Follow the instructions on page 12 to display the icons shown below.

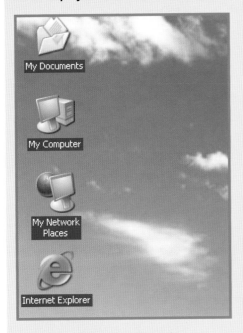

Desktop icons

These icons give you quick access to important areas on your hard disk, the Internet and networked PCs. You can add extra shortcuts to the Desktop for any important files and folders (see page 48), but it's a good idea not to let it

get too cluttered. To access a feature represented by an icon, place your mouse pointer on it and double-click with the left button. Standard Windows XP Desktop icons are featured below.

My Documents

This is the default location for saving your files. To make it work more efficiently for you, learn how to create folders within folders (see page 29). This saves you having to scroll through long lists of files to find the one you want. Windows may automatically create folders within this folder for you, depending on what Windows software you use: My Music is used by Media Player to store your MP3 and other music files; My Pictures is for your images from a scanner or digital camera; and My Received Files stores files you have downloaded from the Internet.

My Computer

You can open all the drives on your computer from this icon, including the floppy disk drive, hard drive, a CD or DVD-ROM drive, and any removable drives. You can then access all of the files and folders inside them by double-clicking the icons.

My Network Places

If your computer is on a network – for example, you may have two or more PCs in your home linked by a communications cable – you can 'see' and access them through this facility. You can then share and transfer files between them, and even share a printer or modem.

Internet Explorer

This lets you browse the Web. You'll need an Internet connection (via a modem or broadband connection to an Internet Service Provider) before you can browse Web pages or send and receive e-mail.

The Recycle Bin

Drag documents into the bin when you have no more use for them. They are stored here until you empty the bin. This allows you to make a final check before you delete them or to bring them back into use.

Bright idea
You can move icons on the Desktop anywhere you want them. By default, they should 'snap' to an invisible grid. If they don't do this, right-click on a blank area of the Desktop, select Arrange Icons By *and put a tick next to 'Align to Grid'.*

Expert advice
Depending on whether you upgraded to or installed Windows XP, your Desktop, its icons and the Taskbar may look slightly different from the images in this book. However, they should all work in the same way.

Moving around a window

There are two types of window that you will see on your Desktop. One is an Explorer window that displays the contents of a disk or folder when its icon is double-clicked. The other is an application window, which opens when you run programs, such as Word or Excel. For ease of use, both types of window have similar features and operate in the same way.

SEE ALSO...
- *Using Windows Explorer* p 24
- *Arranging windows* p 26
- *Change your settings* p 42

A TYPICAL WINDOW
Every windows-compatible program and every Windows folder shares common elements.

The Title bar

Click on the **Start** button and select **My Computer**. The blue strip, called the 'Title bar', at the top of the window tells you the name of the folder (or document) you are viewing, in this case My Computer. The colour

of the Title bar indicates whether the window is active (dark shading) or not (light). You can only work within an active window – to activate an inactive window you simply click on it. To move a window to see and access other items on the Desktop, click on the **Title bar** with the left mouse button and, keeping the button pressed, drag the window. Right-click on the icon in the top-left corner of a folder's Title bar to see a drop-down menu giving access to a range of options, including Windows Explorer (see page 24).

Sizing buttons
On the right of the Title bar, three icons control

the minimize, maximize, restore and close options for that particular window. Click the **Minimize** button

to hide the window. It becomes a button on the Taskbar at the bottom of the screen. To view the window again, just click on this Taskbar button.

Clicking on the Maximize button enlarges the window to fill the entire screen. After this, the button changes from a single square to two overlapping squares,

becoming the Restore Down button. Click on it to return the window to its previous size. On the far right of the

Title bar, you can click on the Close button to shut the window or quit the program.

If you have been working on a document or file and have not saved your work since making some changes, the computer will ask you if you want to save the file before it allows the program to close.

Bright idea
You can maximise a window or restore it to its original size quickly by double-clicking on the window's Title bar.

Watch out
When a program is minimised, a common mistake is to double-click its icon on the Desktop to see it. However, this will open the program again, so that you have two versions running at the same time. To restore a program window, click once on its button on the Taskbar.

WITHIN THE WINDOW
Navigating icons and menus is easy once you know what options are available and where to find them.

Menu bar
The Menu bar displays a series of words that are headings for drop-down menus, each of which lists related commands. Click on a heading to view the menu.

Headings vary, depending on which program window is open, but you will always find commands such as 'Save' and 'Print' under 'File'. Commands for editing content appear under 'Edit'. 'View' helps you manipulate what you see in the window, 'Tools' contains utility commands and 'Help' offers tips and advice relevant to the window or program.

Standard Buttons toolbar
This appears by default just beneath the Menu bar and contains single-click icons for frequently used commands and actions.

The 'Back' and 'Forward' arrows let you cycle through windows you have viewed and the 'Up' button takes you to a higher level of the folder hierarchy. For example, if you are viewing the contents of My Documents, click the **Up** button

to see the Desktop folder in which it is located. The next two options, 'Search' and 'Folders', activate a split pane to the left of the main window. Search lets you look for a particular file by name. Folders accesses files and folders using the structure of the different drives (known as the Directory).

The 'Views' button allows you to quickly change the way your icons are displayed (see 'Change the display', below right). Toolbar options vary in different windows and can be customised to include most command shortcuts (see page 48). To do this, click on the **View** menu, **Toolbars** and then **Customize**.

Address bar
In a Windows or Internet Explorer window, to access an item on your PC, such as a Desktop folder or an Internet address, start typing its name in the address bar and an alphabetically arranged list of files appears automatically. Select the one you want, or type a new address, and click on **Go**.

Task Pane
The 'Task Pane' at the left of a folder or drive window includes links to related tasks, depending on what is selected within the window. If you select a file, you will see options to rename, move, copy, e-mail, print or delete the file. You can also

opt to publish it to a Web site. Each section can be expanded or hidden by clicking the double-arrow button to the right of its heading. A 'Details' section shows the size of the selected item and a preview if it is an image.

Borders and scroll bars

These frame the window, enabling you to resize or scroll around within it. When you place the cursor on the border of a window, it changes to a two-headed arrow. At this point, click and drag to resize the window. Doing this at a corner allows you to resize the width and the height of the window together. Move around the screen to the left and right or up and down by clicking the appropriate arrows on the scroll bars. Or, click and drag the light blue scroll box in the desired direction.

Change the display
Click on the **Views** button to choose how to display the contents of a folder: **Thumbnails** is perfect for pictures as it displays a small version of each image; **Tiles** displays files as large icons with the file type and size; **Icons** are smaller and display no file information; **List** displays the window's contents as tiny icons; and **Details** lists information such as a file's size and creation date. One other option, **Filmstrip**, is only available in picture folders. This displays your images as a row of thumbnails with a large preview area above.

Close up
If you are not sure what a button on a toolbar represents, try letting your mouse pointer hover over it for a second. A small 'ToolTip' message will often appear showing the button's name.

Close up
If you can't see the Address Bar in a Windows folder window, right-click on a Toolbar and put a tick next to Address Bar.

Using the Start menu

The Start button is a fast way to access all of the key programs, documents and files on your PC. By default, it is located in the bottom left-hand corner of the screen. Click on it once to open the Start menu, and then select an item, such as 'Internet', to launch it. The All Programs arrow displays further submenus, containing entries for all the programs on your PC.

SEE ALSO...
- *Personalise your Desktop* p 40
- *Change your settings* p 42
- *User Accounts* p 44

START MENU BASICS

From the Start button you are only ever a couple of clicks away from all the programs and files on your computer.

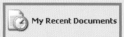 Click on the large green arrow to the right of All Programs to open a submenu. Here you'll see a list of the programs on your PC. Often you'll see a smaller arrow next to a item, such as Accessories. Click on the item to see its submenu. Above All Programs is a quick-access list of your six most recently used programs as well as icons for the Internet and e-mail.

 Select **My Recent Documents** to view a submenu of the last 15 files you worked on. Click on one to open the document in the program that created it.

Click on **Control Panel** to open a window where you can adjust your PC's settings, such as Date and Time, Sounds and Display.

 Use **Printers and Faxes** to add a new printer or set up fax services in Windows with the help of a wizard.

 **Help and Support** has a searchable index of advice. You will need to connect to the Internet to access some information.

 Select **Search** to find files or people in your address book. Turn to page 34 to learn how to use it.

If you have set up your PC for different members of the family (see page 44), you use this option to switch users. Click the **Start** button and select **Log Off**. Then select **Switch User**, choose the new user icon, enter a password, if applicable, and press **Return**.

Close up
If you can't see the 'My Recent Documents' icon on your Start menu, right-click on the **Taskbar and choose** *Properties.* **Then click on the** *Advanced* **tab and put a tick next to 'List my most recently opened documents'.**

A CLOSER LOOK

Familiarise yourself with the 'Turn Off' option, learn how to use 'paths' and customise your Start menu.

Shutting down your computer

Click on the **Start** button and select **Turn Off Computer**. You will see a row of buttons. Choose **Turn Off** to close all programs, save Windows' settings and turn off the PC; or **Restart**, which closes down your computer and then starts it again – this is useful if programs or Windows are not behaving properly. Alternatively, click on **Stand By**, which puts your PC to 'sleep' to save power. Moving the mouse or pressing a key will wake it up.

Use the Run feature

By selecting **Run**, you can launch anything you have on your machine, including programs and music CDs. You can even access the Internet by typing in a Web address and clicking **OK**.

If you know where the item you want to launch is situated on your computer, you can type in the route you have to take to get to the file, known as the 'path', and then click **OK** to access the file. For instance, the path to the program WinZip might be 'C:\Program Files\WinZip'. 'C:' is the drive that WinZip is on, while 'Program Files' is the folder in which WinZip resides. If you don't know the path to the file you want to open, click the **Browse** button to search your computer for it.

Customise the Start menu

To adapt the Start menu to your needs, right-click on a blank section of the Taskbar and select **Properties** from the pop-up menu. Click on the **Start Menu** tab and then on the **Customize** button.

Select the **General** tab to switch between large and small icons on the Start menu, and to choose the number of program icons that will

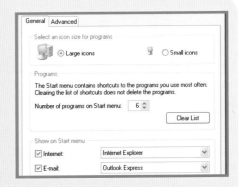

be visible and whether to show Internet Explorer and Outlook Express at the top of the menu. Select the **Advanced** tab to choose whether submenus open when you pause the mouse pointer over a menu item and whether you want Windows to highlight newly installed programs so you can find them quickly. Under these items is a list of options. Scroll through to see what you can do. For instance, if you would like to add a submenu to the Control Panel, put a dot next to 'Display as a menu'. When you're finished, click **OK** and then **OK** again.

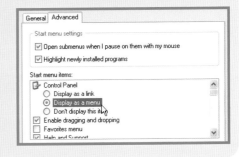

Bright idea
If you want to add a frequently used program to the top section of the Start menu, drag it from its program menu to the Start button and then up to the required position.

Close up
You may see slightly different options on the 'Turn off computer' screen. Some PCs have a 'Hibernate' feature, which allows them to shut down but save the state of your open applications so that, when you restart your PC, the Desktop is restored just as you left it.

Using Windows Explorer

Unlike previous versions of Windows, every time you open a folder or double-click on a disk drive in Windows XP, the window that opens includes the Windows Explorer tools and features. This facility not only allows you to access your file and folder system easily and efficiently, but also helps you to organise and sort the files in a way that suits your needs.

SEE ALSO...
● *File your work* p 28
● *Finding files* p 34

FINDING YOUR WAY AROUND

To access the Windows Explorer tools, click on the Start menu and choose My Documents. Then click on the Folders button on the Toolbar.

What you see

A typical Explorer window is divided into two panes. On the left-hand side is a list of the drives and folders on your PC. When you click on one of these, the files and folders it contains are displayed in the right-hand pane. This means that you can search through the entire contents of your computer in a single window.

The left-hand pane is for navigating around your computer. Click on the small plus sign (+) to the left of a drive or a folder to see the subfolders contained in that drive or folder. Click on the minus sign (-) to hide the subfolders again. This makes it much easier to scroll through the list when you're looking for your files. If there is no plus or minus sign, that folder contains only files, which are displayed in the right-hand pane

when you click on the folder. Click on a folder or file in the right-hand pane and click the **Folders** button to see a summarised description of that selected item under **Details**. The summary will tell you what the item is, when it was last modified, its size and, if it is a file, the name of the original author.

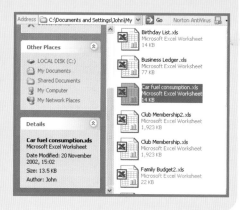

Bright idea
If you regularly work on the same file, right-click on it in any folder window and select Send To, then Desktop (create shortcut). This places a shortcut icon on the Desktop which, when double-clicked, will open your file.

LOOKING CLOSER

When you are familiar with Windows Explorer, it is easy to navigate your hard disk and reorganise your files.

Sorting files and folders

There are five main ways to view the data on the right-hand side of the Explorer window: Thumbnails, Tiles, Icon, List and Details. To select an option, click on the **View** menu or click the **Views** button on the right of the toolbar (see page 21 for information). Select **Details** for the most comprehensive viewing option – you'll see the file name, size and type, and the date and time it was last saved.

If you choose to view your files and folders by 'Details' or 'Icons', you can alter the order in which they are displayed. Click on the **View** menu and then **Arrange Icons by**. The submenu gives you several options:
Name displays files in alphabetical order, with the folders grouped together at the top or bottom of the list – the order can be changed by clicking the small arrow next to Name.
Size arranges folders by name in ascending alphabetical order, and then files by size, with the smallest file first.
Type groups files of the same kind – such as graphics files or Word documents – in ascending alphabetical order. Folders are placed at the bottom of the list.
Modified sorts folders and files with the most recently modified files at the top.
Show in Groups organises the files according to which column heading is selected. If you choose the Type heading then the files are grouped by the program they were created in. If you choose Name then they are grouped alphabetically by name. Modified organises the files by the date they were last saved.

Changing views

If you choose the Details view and have not selected the Show in Groups option, you'll see that the sort order is indicated by a small arrow beside the column heading. You can sort your files by a different category by clicking on a column heading in the Name bar. Clicking on the heading again reverses the sort order.

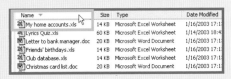

Organising your work

Folders are a good way to group your files together. To create a new folder, choose where you want it to go by clicking once on the appropriate folder or drive icon in the left-hand pane of Explorer. Now click on the **File** menu and select **New**, then **Folder**. A new folder

icon appears in the right-hand pane with the name 'New Folder' highlighted. Type a folder name and press **Return**. You can now drag and drop files into this folder. In the right pane, locate the file you want to put in the new folder. Then find your folder in the left pane, by opening other folders until you can see it. Don't click on the folder you want. Click on the file on the right and drag it onto your folder's icon on the left. When the folder is highlighted, release the mouse button to complete the action.

Customising folders

You can change the appearance of folders in Windows Explorer to help identify files belonging to different users. Open the folder you want to change. Click on the **View** menu and select **Customize This Folder**. You can choose a picture to go on your folder, or change the icon to make it more recognisable. The picture will only be visible in Thumbnails view though.

Arranging windows

The Windows Desktop can easily become filled with open program and folder windows – for example, a letter in progress, your e-mail Inbox, or a spreadsheet of monthly expenses. However, with a little organisation, you can resize and switch between windows quickly and easily, and still stay focused on the task in hand.

SEE ALSO...
- *Using the Start menu p 22*
- *Using Windows Explorer p 24*
- *Create your own shortcuts p 48*

BEFORE YOU START
Open up a few windows on your Desktop, such as a letter, an e-mail program, and your My Documents folder. You can experiment with them as you go through the steps.

1 If you need to move a window to a different position on your screen, so you can see it while working in another window, for instance, click on the **Title bar** at the top of the window and drag it to wherever you want. If your windows are the wrong size, you can resize them by clicking on any of the corners or sides; the mouse pointer turns into a double-headed arrow and you can then drag windows inwards or outwards to the new size.

2 The easiest way to work with multiple windows is to have only one visible at a time. If there are any windows you are not using, click on their **Minimize** buttons (in the upper right-hand corner). Each minimised window appears as a button on the Taskbar. If you have six or more documents open in the same program, their Taskbar buttons will be reduced to one button with the number of windows on it. Click on it and a list pops up.

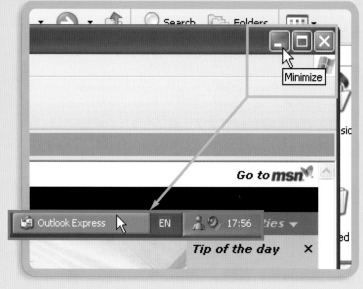

Customise your Taskbar

You can move your Taskbar to the sides or top of your screen. Click on the **Taskbar** near, but not on, the Start button, and drag it to where you want. To make the Taskbar bigger, position the mouse on the line between

the top of the Taskbar and the Desktop (left). When it changes into a double-headed arrow, click and drag the **Taskbar** upwards. Note, you need to unlock the Taskbar first, see page 13.

That's amazing!
Right-click on the **Taskbar** and select **Toolbars** to choose from a range of options. You can convert your Desktop icons to buttons on the Taskbar, show an Address bar for Web addresses, or even display a list of Internet links.

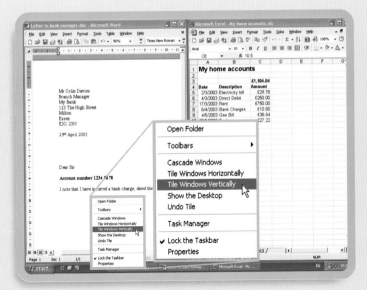

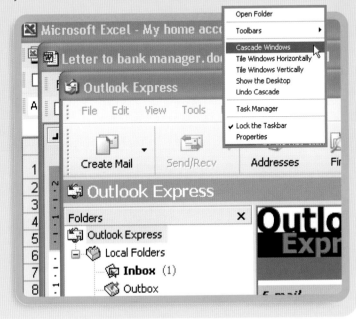

4 If you have three or more windows open, right-click on the **Taskbar** and select **Cascade Windows**. This makes the windows overlap slightly so you can view all the Title bars at once (below). Or, to clear the Desktop of all windows, click on the **Show Desktop** button and all the windows will instantly be reduced to buttons on your Taskbar.

3 If you're working with two related documents in different programs, it can help to have the two windows side by side on screen. To do this, open both documents, right-click on the **Taskbar** and choose **Tile Windows Vertically**. You can now work in either window simply by clicking anywhere in it. Note that if you choose 'Tile Windows Horizontally', the windows will occupy the top and bottom halves of the Windows Desktop.

File your work

Your hard disk is like a virtual filing cabinet: each document is stored in a folder, as are all the programs you use. Also, folders can be stored in other folders, like drawers in the cabinet. It's tempting to keep all your documents on your Windows Desktop where you can see them but, as with a real desk, life is much easier if you avoid clutter and confusion.

SEE ALSO...
- *What is Windows?* p 12
- *Using Windows Explorer* p 24
- *Deleting files* p 32
- *Maintain your hard disk* p 76

CREATING FOLDERS
There are several ways to create new folders. The method you use depends on how and where you save your work. Here are three ways to make a new folder.

1 Always create new folders for your work within the My Documents folder, or in a folder inside My Documents, such as My Pictures. First click on the **Start** button and choose **My Documents**. Then click on the **File** menu and select **New** then **Folder**. If you want to save in a folder within My Documents, double-click on the appropriate folder before creating a new folder.

2 Your new folder will appear in the right pane. The highlighted name, 'New Folder', is the default name and will be replaced as soon as you begin typing in your preferred folder name. Choose a recognisable and memorable name for your new folder and press **Return**.

Finding lost files

If you can't find a file or folder, click on the **Start** menu, select **Search** then **All Files or Folders**. Type the file name, or as much of it as you can remember, in the box under 'All or part of the file name'. Click on the **Search** button to begin the search. The results are displayed in the right pane.

Expert advice

Always name your files logically so that if you forget a file's full name, you can still perform a search for it. If several family members use your PC, and you haven't set up 'User Accounts' (see page 44), you can create folders for each person. Use names or initials when naming documents to distinguish one person's files from another.

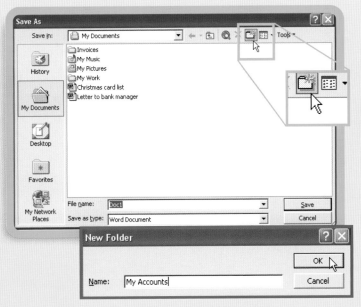

3 You can also create a new folder within the My Documents folder while you are saving. Open a document, click on **File** and choose **Save As**. In the Save As dialogue box click on the **Create New Folder** button. In the New Folder dialogue box give the folder a name, then click on **OK**. Double-click on your new folder and click on the **Save** button to store your document.

4 Alternatively, you can create new folders in any folder window by using your right mouse button. Open the folder in which you want to create your new folder. Then right-click on a blank area, select **New** and choose **Folder**. The default name on the folder that appears will be replaced as you type in the new name.

Copy and move files

There are many reasons why you may need to copy or move a file or folder – you may want to make a backup of an important document, or perhaps you need to copy files to a floppy disk so that you can transfer them to another PC. Maybe you just want to move a file to another folder on your hard disk. Whatever you want to do, Windows makes it easy.

SEE ALSO...
- *Using Windows Explorer* p 24
- *File your work* p 28

BEFORE YOU START
To copy to a floppy disk, follow the first three steps. To copy to your hard disk, open My Documents, then click the **Folders** button and follow the steps on page 31.

COPYING TO A FLOPPY

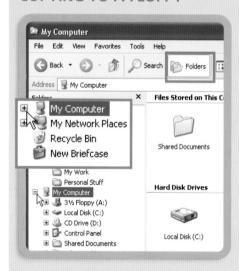

1 To copy a file to a floppy disk, first insert a blank disk into the drive, then click on the **Start** button and select **My Documents**. Click on the **Folders** button and the My Documents window divides in two. Click on the + sign to the left of the My Computer icon to open a list of drives.

2 The right pane displays the files and folders you can copy. Locate the one you want to copy by opening folders. Click on it and, keeping your finger pressed down on the mouse button, drag it onto the **3½ Floppy (A:)** drive icon in the left pane. When the icon becomes highlighted, release the mouse button.

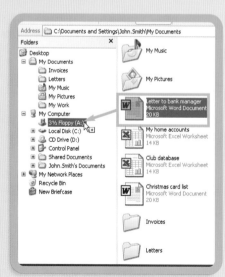

3 A dialogue box opens to show the copying operation in progress and will automatically close once it is finished. If you realise that you are copying the wrong file, or the right file to the wrong folder, click on **Cancel** and copying will be stopped.

Moving files

As with a conventional paper filing system, you will often want to move your files and folders. Windows helps with this. Click on the file or folder and, keeping your finger pressed down on the left mouse button, drag it over to the new location. When the destination folder is highlighted, release the mouse button and the file or folder will move.

Watch out

When you drag a file from one drive to another, for example, from your hard disk to the floppy drive, you are left with two identical files: one on the original drive and an exact copy on the destination drive. If you drag a file to a different place on the same drive, the file will just move, without making a copy.

MAKING COPIES OF FILES

1 To make a copy of a file that is stored on your hard disk, first open the folder that contains the file that you wish to copy. Then click on the file once to select it, click on the **Edit** menu and select **Copy**.

2 Now locate the folder into which you wish to paste a copy of the selected file. Double-click on it, then click on the **Edit** menu and select **Paste**. An exact copy of the file will appear in the right-hand pane of the window.

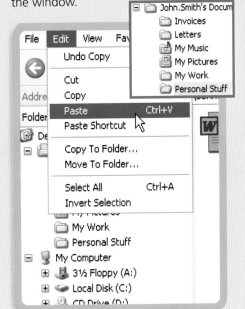

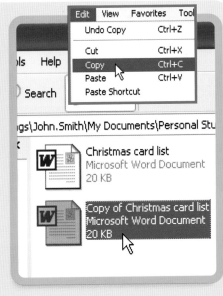

3 You can also store a copy of a file within the same folder as the original. Click on the relevant file, click on the **Edit** menu, select **Copy** and then click on **Edit** again followed by **Paste**. To distinguish the copy, Windows names the new file 'Copy of' followed by the name of your original file.

Deleting files

Regardless of how fast or powerful your computer is, if its hard disk gets too full it will begin to slow down and there will be less disk space available for new files and programs. You should regularly delete redundant personal files and folders from your hard disk by moving them to the Recycle Bin. This then needs to be emptied to free up the disk space.

SEE ALSO...
- *Maximise your disk space* p 72
- *Uninstall old programs* p 74
- *Maintain your hard disk* p 76

THROWING ITEMS AWAY

It's easy to dump unwanted files or folders in the Recycle Bin. And if you throw one away by mistake, you can retrieve it just as quickly.

Delete options

There are a number of ways to put a item in the Recycle Bin: you can drag and drop the file or folder onto the Bin icon; select the file and press the **Delete** key on the keyboard; or right-click on the file and choose **Delete**. When you choose to delete a file (unless you drag it to the bin),

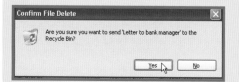

Windows will ask you if you are sure you want to do this. Click on the **Yes** button to confirm the action. Note, the bin icon will be hidden if you are in a maximised window, so you will not be able to use the drag and drop method to delete an item.

The Desktop icon shows an empty bin when there is nothing in it and displays contents in the bin when it contains files. You can view the contents of the Recycle Bin by double-clicking on it. Putting files in the bin does not free up disk space, as the files are still stored on your hard drive. In order to free up the space, you

must empty the Recycle Bin. With the Recycle Bin window open, you can see a list of its contents, with options for emptying the Bin and restoring files on the left of the screen (if these options are not visible, click the **Folders** button). Choose **Empty the Recycle Bin** to permanently delete all the files. If you do not want to delete all the files in one go, select the ones you know that you no longer want, click on the **File** menu and choose **Delete**. You will need to confirm your action.

Restoring files

Select **Restore all items** in the left of the Recycle Bin window to return the files to their original locations on your PC. If you only want to restore one file, select it and click on the **Restore this item** button.

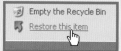

Bright idea
If you want to delete a few files at the same time, select them all by clicking on the first file, holding down the Ctrl key and the clicking on the others in turn. You can then delete them collectively using the methods described above.

Watch out
Files deleted from a floppy disk or other removable storage media will not be placed in the Recycle Bin. Also files too large for the Bin will be deleted immediately. If this is the case, Windows will display a warning box.

THE RECYCLE BIN PROPERTIES

The storage capacity of the Recycle Bin can be increased or decreased to suit your requirements – but you may need to take the size of your hard drive into consideration.

Adjusting the capacity of the bin

Right-click on the **Recycle Bin** icon, choose **Properties** and click on the **Global** tab. Here you can determine just what proportion of the hard disk you are prepared to allocate to the storage of files in the Recycle Bin.

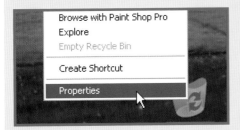

It is unlikely that you would ever need to set the range above 10 per cent (the default) of your hard disk, but you can set it at anything up to 100 per cent. You should bear in mind that if you choose a very high percentage, you must empty the Recycle Bin regularly or it will gradually fill up your hard disk. This may result in your PC slowing down and eventually you will receive a warning that disk space is low.

To change the setting, just drag the slider to the left or right and click on **OK**. When this limit is reached, your PC will automatically

begin to delete the files in the bin, starting with the oldest ones. If you work with lots of large files, you may want to increase the setting to 25% to allow for their storage.

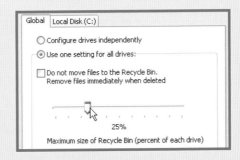

Deliberate deletion

If you wish, you can get rid of the Confirm File Delete dialogue box that appears when you move a file or folder to the bin. In the Recycle Bin Properties dialogue box, remove the tick next to 'Display delete confirmation dialog', then click

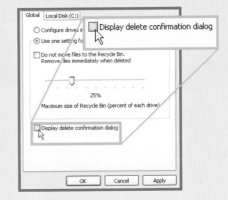

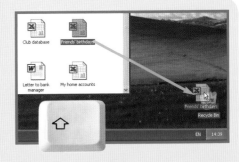

on **Apply** and **OK**. Your files or folders will now go straight into the Recycle Bin. If you are sure that you will never need a file again, hold down the **Shift** key when you drag it into the Recycle Bin (above). The Confirm File Delete dialogue box does not appear and the file is deleted without being held in the bin.

Alternatively, you can put a tick next to 'Do not move files to the Recycle Bin. Remove files immediately when deleted' in the Recycle Bin Properties box. Only use these methods if you are confident that you no longer need your documents because, once you have done this, the files can only be recovered with the help of specialist software, such as Norton Utilities.

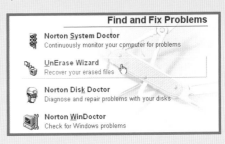

That's amazing!

Hard disks on even the most basic computer now come with a 20GB or 40GB hard disk, but on more expensive models they can be as much as 80GB or 120GB. Unless you are editing a movie on your PC, it is unlikely that these large disks will ever be filled. Nonetheless, it is good practice to delete old files on a regular basis.

Finding files

Once you have been using your computer for a while you may build up a large collection of files and programs. Even with an efficient filing system, it is possible you may not be able to find a document that you need. Windows XP's Search facility not only allows you to locate files on your PC, but also enables you to find Web sites and information via the Internet.

SEE ALSO...
- *Using Windows Explorer* p 24
- *File your work* p 28

THE SEARCH IS ON

Regardless of how many files are stored on your PC, Windows can locate any one of them quickly – even if you're not sure of the file name.

Locating files

If you are having trouble finding a specific file, the first place to look for it is in the My Documents folder. If you can remember in which folder you normally save your work – for instance, 'Letters' or 'Personal Stuff' – then that's the first place to look.

If your file isn't there, and you know that it was worked on recently, click on the **Start** button and then on **My Recent Documents**. This lists the last 15 files that were opened on your computer, even if you made no changes to them. If the file you want is listed, click on it once to open it. If neither of these methods proves successful, you may have accidentally saved your file in the wrong folder or dragged it to the Recycle Bin. In this case you will need to use the Windows Search tool.

Windows' Search facility

To open Search, click on the **Start** button, then on **Search**. Or hold down the **Windows** key and press the **F** key on your keyboard.

There are four options available in the Search Task Pane:

Pictures, music, or video
Use this option to search for images and photographs, music files and videos.

Documents
This lets you search for word processor, spreadsheet and other documents, according to when they were last modified.

All files and folders
This enables you to look for any type of file or folder stored on your hard disk.

Computers or people
Use this to look up contact details stored in your Address Book, or to search for computers connected to yours.

Close up
If you click on the Search button on any folder toolbar, it opens the Search For Files and Folders facility in the left-hand pane of the folder window.

That's amazing!
If you have forgotten a file's full name, you can use the '*' symbol (type **Shift + 8**) to search for it. When you use the asterisk in a search, it represents any character or characters in the file name. If you only know that your file name started with an 'S', type '**s***', or if your file is a Word file that ends with the name 'john', type '***john.doc**'.

WINDOWS' SEARCHES

Some files are easier to find than others, so try a basic search first. If that doesn't work, use the advanced search.

Basic search

Click on the **Start** button and select **Search** then **All Files and Folders**. The first box lets

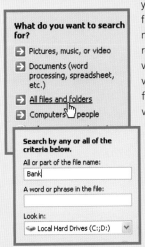

you type in the file or folder name, if you can remember it. Be warned: Search will retrieve any files with this word in it so if you type in 'count', it will also find 'account', 'accountant' and 'accountancy'. You can also filter results by specifying some text from the file in the 'A word or phrase in the file' box. So, if you know that your home address is part of the document that you are looking for, type the first line in this box. Windows then reads through all the corresponding files, making it a useful, but slow, search option. Below this, the 'Look in' box helps to speed up the search by telling your computer where to look. If you know the file is

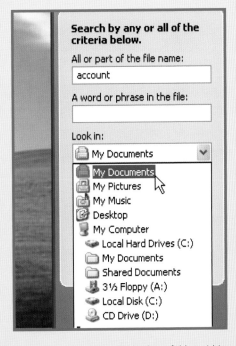

in your My Documents folder (or a folder within My Documents), for instance, click the down arrow to the right of the 'Look in' panel and click on **My Documents**. This is quicker than searching the entire computer, and could turn up more specific results.

When the search is complete, a list of results appears on the right of the screen. If you see the file you want, double-click on its name to open it. You can always stop a search from progressing if you spot the file you need in the results list. Just click on the **Stop** button.

Advanced search

To customise your search further, click on one of the options below 'Look in':

When was it modified? – this is useful if you know roughly when the file was last saved.

What size is it? – searches on the basis of file size, so if you are looking for a large image you can search for all files over, say, 1MB.

More advanced options – lets you search system folders and hidden files and folders. You can also choose not to look in subfolders if you know the file is in a specific folder or drive.

Case sensitive – this means it will look for exactly the same capital or lowercase letters as those you've typed into the Search panel.

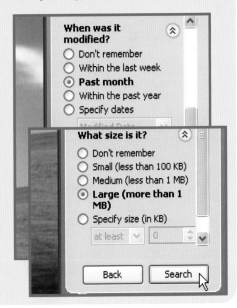

Sorting your results

When a search is complete, your results will be listed in the order in which Search located them. This is because Search looks in a specific sequence of locations. Click on the **Name bar** above the file names to see the results listed alphabetically with folders first, followed by any relevant files that start with a number. Click on the **Name bar** again to view the results in reverse alphabetical order.

Using Briefcase

I f you often work on more than one computer, Briefcase is
ideal for making sure your documents are always up to date.
It is a virtual briefcase, an effective means of moving files
between your workplace and your home, or to a PC or laptop
elsewhere. It ensures that you are always working on the most
recent version of a file, whichever computer you use.

SEE ALSO...
- *Using Windows Explorer* p 24
- *File your work* p 28

BEFORE YOU START
You will need a floppy, Zip or
CD-RW disk. To create a new

Briefcase, right-click on the
Desktop, and click on **New**
followed by **Briefcase**.

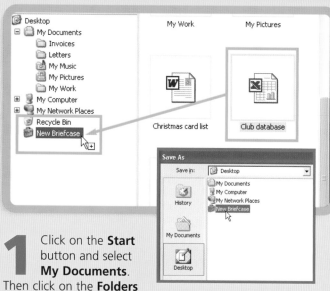

1 Click on the **Start**
button and select
My Documents.
Then click on the **Folders**
button, if necessary, to see
the folders in the left pane.
Select the files you wish to
transfer from the right pane,
and drag them onto the **New
Briefcase** icon in the left
pane. Alternatively, you can
save a document straight into

the Briefcase from a program.
Open a document, click on
the **File** menu then **Save as**.
Click **Desktop** in the list on
the left and double-click on
New Briefcase. Now name
your file in the box next to
'File name' and click on **Save**.

2 Next, insert a disk into
the relevant drive.
Double-click on **My
Computer** in the left pane
and click once on the correct
icon for your drive. To copy
the files in New Briefcase onto
your chosen disk, click on the
New Briefcase icon in the

left hand pane and drag it
into the right hand pane.
   When it has finished
copying, the New Briefcase
icon will disappear from the
left pane (and your Desktop)
and appear in your chosen
drive window. You can now
remove the disk.

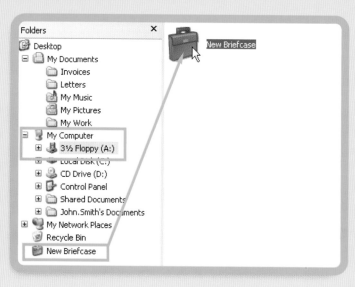

Bright idea
To select a long list of files, click on the first one, hold down the Shift key and click on the last one in the list. All the files in between will be highlighted automatically.

Expert advice
You can use Briefcase to synchronise files by connecting a laptop directly to your desktop PC. Just copy the files from the PC to the New Briefcase on your laptop. You can then take your laptop away to work on the files. When you bring it back, synchronise the files by reconnecting the two machines and following step 4 below.

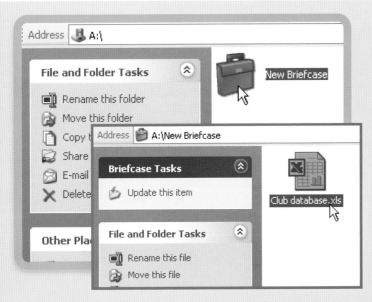

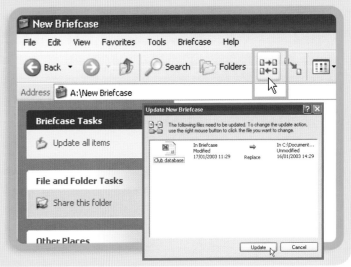

4 Open My Computer and double-click the drive icon on which the New Briefcase is stored, then on the **New Briefcase** icon. Click the **Update All** button on the toolbar. In the Update New Briefcase dialogue box, click on **Update**. Your PC now updates the original file versions on its hard drive. For more information about files stored in the Briefcase, click on the **View** menu and select **Details**. You'll be able to see where on your computer the synchronised copies are stored and whether they are up to date.

3 Insert your disk into the other computer. Click on the **Start** button and select **My Computer**, and then click on the appropriate drive icon for your disk. Double-click on the **New Briefcase** icon to access your documents and then open and work on them as usual. Don't forget to save before closing your files. To synchronise your modified files, first take the disk out of the drive, and reinsert it in the drive of your main computer.

Quick keyboard commands

Nearly all the actions or commands you perform with your mouse can also be done by pressing 'hot keys' – these are single keys or combinations of keys. For example, you can access the Start menu by pressing the 'Windows' key at the bottom left of your keyboard, or you can open My Computer by pressing the 'Windows' and 'E' keys together.

HANDY HOT KEYS
Select menu options and navigate Windows using key commands.

Selecting main menu options
The menu bars in Windows and programs such as Word look very similar. They contain common menus such as File, Edit and View. In program windows, one letter is underlined in each menu item, for example, 'File' or 'Format'. In Windows Explorer you have to press the **Alt** key (to the left of the Spacebar on the keyboard) to see these letters. In any window, press **Alt** followed by the underlined letter in the menu item to open the menu:

- **Alt** + **F** to open the File menu
- **Alt** + **E** to open the Edit menu
- **Alt** + **V** to open the View menu
- **Alt** + **A** to open the Favorites menu
- **Alt** + **T** to open the Tools menu
- **Alt** + **H** to open the Help menu.

Using the Function keys
The Function keys, also known as the 'F keys', at the top of the keyboard perform preset actions. For example, press **F1** to access a program's Help database. From the Windows Desktop, press **F3** to access the Search Results dialogue box. You can also use Function keys in combination with other keys. To close a window or program, for example, press the **Alt** and **F4** keys together.

Moving around the Desktop
You can use keyboard shortcuts to move around your Desktop. For example, click anywhere on the Desktop, then press the arrow keys to move to any icon (they are highlighted when selected). Press the **Return** or **Enter** key to open the selected item.

The same principle can be applied inside folders. Open the My Documents folder then press the arrow keys to move around the folder's contents. Press **Return** when you want to open a selected file or folder.

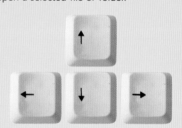

Important command keys

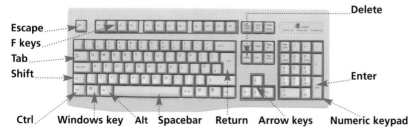

Escape · F keys · Tab · Shift · Delete · Enter

Ctrl · Windows key · Alt · Spacebar · Return · Arrow keys · Numeric keypad

Close up
If several programs are open, use the Alt and Tab keys to choose which is active. Hold down Alt and then press Tab and a bar shows the program icons – the active one is outlined. Move through the icons by pressing Tab, and release Alt to make the outlined program active.

Customising Windows

Personalise your Desktop

The Windows Desktop is part of your working environment and so it is important you like its appearance and colour scheme. Fortunately, you can change the background image on the Windows Desktop and the colour of the window frames with just a few clicks. And you can choose from a range of animated screen savers for when you're not using your PC.

SEE ALSO...
- *Change your settings* p 42
- *Create your own shortcuts* p 48

DESKTOP MAKEOVER
Windows comes with an extensive selection of Desktop backgrounds.

Background images
To change your Desktop background, right-click anywhere on your **Desktop** and select **Properties** from the pop-up menu. In the Display Properties dialogue box, select the **Desktop** tab and scroll through the list of images under 'Background'. Click on any that interest you and view them in the preview window (right), then click on the **Apply** button to see how they look on the Desktop. When you've made your choice, click on **OK**. If the image doesn't fill your screen, go back into the Display Properties dialogue box. Click on the down arrow under 'Position' to open the

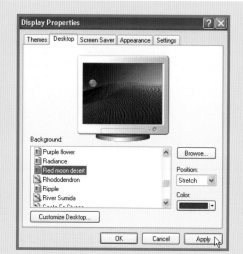

drop-down list, select **Tile** to repeat the image over your Desktop, **Stretch** to force the image to fit the screen (above) or **Center** to position it in the centre of the Desktop.

USING YOUR OWN PICTURES
You can use your own digital photographs, stored on the hard disk, as your Desktop background.

A truly personal Desktop
Make sure you store any pictures you have downloaded, scanned or taken using a digital camera in your My Pictures folder – you will find My Pictures in the My Documents folder. Your pictures will then be available for selection from the 'Background' list in the Display Properties dialogue box automatically.

If you want to use pictures stored in another folder, open the Display Properties box and, under the **Desktop** tab, click on the **Browse** button. Locate your photograph, select it, and click on **Open**. Then select the image from the 'Background' list. Click on **Apply** and then **OK** to confirm your choice.

Bright idea
Remind yourself of an important message using a screen saver. In the Display Properties dialogue box, **select the** Screen Saver **tab, choose the** Marquee **screen saver and click on the** Settings **button. Then type your reminder, and select a font, colour and style. Choose how fast it scrolls across your screen, then click on** OK **and** OK **again.**

MOVING PICTURES

Screen savers are animations that appear when your PC is idle. They can also protect work from prying eyes.

Small screen animation

To select a screen saver, right-click anywhere on the **Desktop** and select **Properties** from the pop-up menu. Click on the **Screen Saver** tab and then click on the down arrow to the right of the box under 'Screen saver'. Scroll through the list and select an option.

COLOUR SCHEMES

Windows lets you choose different colour schemes for your Desktop.

More than just a Desktop

Open the Display Properties dialogue box and click on the **Appearance** tab. Under 'Color Scheme' you can choose from three sets of Windows colours: 'Blue' (the default), 'Olive Green' (shown above) and 'Silver'. Click on **Apply** to see how each one looks.

Click on **Effects** for more options – you can smooth your onscreen fonts, select larger icons for your Desktop and put shadows under your menus. If you prefer to see your menus and

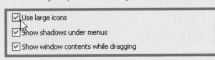

buttons displayed in the Windows Me style, click on the drop-down list under 'Windows and Buttons' and choose **Windows Classic style**.

Click on **Preview** to view your choice on screen. Then simply move the mouse and the Display Properties dialogue box reappears. Set the length of time your PC waits before activating the screen saver in the 'Wait' box. Finally, click on **OK** to confirm your choices.

Save your energy

On some PCs, the Screen Saver tab in the Display Properties dialogue box has an energy-saving option that reduces the amount of power used by your monitor and/or hard disk after a set period of inactivity. Click on the **Power** button and the Power Options Properties dialogue box opens. Click on the down arrow to the right of the 'Turn off monitor' and 'Turn off hard disks' panels and select appropriate timescales from the lists.

Change your settings

Whether it's just for fun or to make using your PC more comfortable, you can adjust many of Windows' settings to suit your needs. It's possible to alter the speed at which the mouse pointer moves and how fast you must double-click to launch an item. You can also set a series of sounds that are triggered in response to your actions.

SEE ALSO...
- *Personalise your Desktop p 40*
- *User Accounts p 44*

USEFUL SETTINGS
By customising a few settings you can make sure that your PC works just the way you want it to.

Mouse settings
To customise your mouse settings, click on the **Start** button and then **Control Panel**.

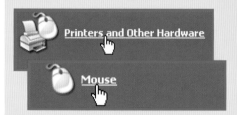

Click on **Printers and Other Hardware** and then click on the **Mouse** icon. See the 'Close up' tip below if your Control Panel shows different options.

There are four tabs at the top of the Mouse Properties dialogue box:
Buttons allows left-handed users to swap the function of the mouse buttons from left to right. You can also adjust the double-click speed of your mouse under 'Double-click speed'. To test the setting, double-click on the folder – if it opens and closes, the speed is right for you. If not, drag the slider towards 'Slow'.

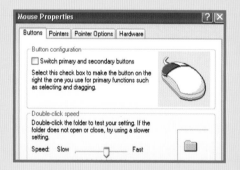

Pointers lets you change your mouse pointers – double-click the pointer you want to change, choose from the range displayed and click the **Open** button. Or you can change all the pointers using one of the built-in schemes from the drop-down list under 'Scheme'.
Pointer Options enables you to alter the speed at which the pointer moves in relation to the movement of the mouse, and choose whether

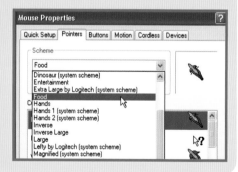

Close up
Depending on how your PC is set up, the Control Panel window may be displayed in 'Category view' (the default, shown above), or in 'Classic view' (Windows Me style). Click on Switch to Category View *if your Control Panel looks different from the pictures above.*

Watch out
If your PC came with a non-standard mouse, or you have upgraded your mouse, the Mouse Properties dialogue box may look slightly different from the one shown here. However, all the features will be present, and there may even be some advanced settings for the extra buttons.

you want the pointer to automatically snap to buttons ready for you to click, and whether the mouse leaves a **cursor trail** and is hidden while you type.

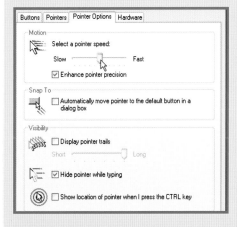

Hardware allows you to check whether your mouse has the right drivers installed, and to launch a Windows troubleshooting wizard to help you resolve problems with your mouse.

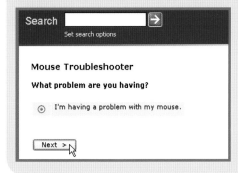

Date and time

The current time is displayed on the right-hand side of the Taskbar. To see the date, hover your mouse pointer over the time display. To set the date or time, double-click on the time display. Click on the hour, minutes or seconds in the box and then on the up or down arrows to adjust each setting.

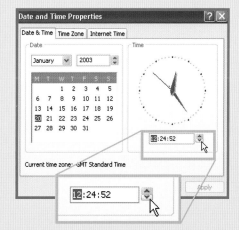

To set the time zone for your location, click on the **Time Zone** tab and then on the down arrow to the right of the 'Time Zone' panel. Scroll down the list and click on your zone.

Windows can also be set so that it switches between British Summer Time and GMT automatically on the correct dates. To do this, put a tick next to 'Automatically adjust clock for daylight saving changes' and click on **Apply** followed by **OK**.

Setting sounds

You can configure Windows to play sounds to accompany a particular event. Click on the **Start** button, select **Control Panel**, click on the **Sounds, Speech and Audio Devices** icon and click **Sounds and Audio Devices**. Select the **Sounds** tab and choose an event from the 'Program events' list. Click on the down arrow to the right of the 'Sounds' box and select your preferred sound. To hear a sound, click on the arrow button beside the 'Sounds' box.

If you wish, you can load one of Windows' preset sound schemes. Click on the down arrow to the right of the 'Sound scheme' box and choose the scheme you like. You can adjust the volume of these sounds on the 'Sound Volume' slider under the 'Volume' tab.

Key word
A cursor trail is a series of 'ghost' images left by your mouse pointer when you move it around the screen. It is designed to make the pointer easier to see on certain types of monitor.

That's amazing!
Your PC clock is built into the motherboard and runs even when your PC is turned off. Windows XP makes sure your computer's clock is always accurate by checking its time against a computer on the Internet. If there's a difference, Windows updates your PC's clock.

User Accounts

Windows XP is designed to make sharing your computer easy and secure. If several family members want to use the same PC, you can set up individual 'User Accounts' to allow each person to customise their Desktop and have their own list of favourite Internet sites. You should password-protect each account so only the correct user can access it.

SEE ALSO...
● *Personalise your Desktop* p 40

NEW USERS

Creating User Accounts in Windows XP is easy – you can decide whether a user can install and remove programs or simply access their files.

You must be logged in as an administrator (an account with full access rights) to set up a new user. Click on the **Start** button, select **Control Panel** and click on **User Accounts**. (If your Control Panel looks different from the pictures below, see the 'Close up' tip on page 42 to

change the view.) Then click on the **Create a new account** link. Under 'Name the new

Name the new account

Type a name for the new account:

Janet

This name will appear on the Welcome screen and on the Start menu.

account', type a name for your new user and click on the **Next** button. At the next screen, choose whether you want your account type to be 'Computer administrator' with full access rights, or 'Limited', with access only to certain applications, files and settings. Then click on the

○ Computer administrator ● Limited

With a limited account, you can:
- Change or remove your password
- Change your picture, theme, and other desktop settings
- View files you created
- View files in the Shared Documents folder

Create Account button. You are returned to the User Accounts screen where the new user has been allocated an icon. If you change your mind, you can alter these settings after you've set up the account. You should always password protect administrator accounts.

Close up
If you want to control your children's access to sexually explicit or violent material on Web sites, you can set up Internet preferences for them. Open Control Panel, go to Network and Internet Connections and select Internet Options. Select the Content tab and click on the Enable button under 'Content Advisor' to set the ratings.

Watch out
If you are the only Computer administrator and you forget your password you will no longer be able to access many of Windows' features. To avoid this problem, create a 'password reset disk'. Open **User Accounts** in **Control Panel** and select your account name. Then click on **Prevent a forgotten password** under 'Related Tasks' on the left and follow the steps in the Forgotten Password Wizard.

MANAGING ACCOUNTS
Each user can have an individual picture and can choose a password so no-one else can access their files.

If you want to change the image Windows has allocated to your account, click once on the account in the User Accounts window. Then click on the **Change the picture** link. Either choose a new image from a list, or browse your hard disk for one of your own pictures.

To password-protect a user's account, first click on the account you want to change and then click on the **Create a password** link. At the next screen you must enter the password twice, to confirm you have spelt it correctly.

LOG ON OPTIONS
You can log on to Windows using the Welcome screen or type both the user name and password for added security.

When you start Windows, you will see a Welcome screen, displaying a list of all the users on your PC. Click on your user name, type a password (if required) and click the green arrow button to log on to Windows.

For added security, you can be prompted for your user name and a password by a dialogue box before the Windows Desktop appears. In the User Accounts window, click on **Change the way users log on or off** and remove the tick next to 'Use the Welcome screen'. Then click on the **Apply Options** button. When you next start Windows, you'll be asked to enter your user name and password in a dialogue box and click on the **OK** button.

FAST USER SWITCHING
If you regularly need to swap users, you can use Fast User Switching to allow people to log on and off while leaving their programs running.

Put a tick next to 'Use Fast User Switching' on the Select logon and logoff options screen and click on **Apply Options**. Then, when you click on the **Start** button and select **Log Off**, you will see a screen asking if you want to 'Log Off' or 'Switch User'. Click on the **Switch User** button. Windows stores the state of all your programs and windows and allows a second

user to log on to a new default Desktop by clicking on their icon and typing their password. When the second user is finished, they choose **Log Off** from the **Start** menu and then either click **Log Off**, if they have finished working for the day, or **Switch User**. You can then click on your icon and enter your password to restore your Desktop exactly as you left it. Users should always choose the 'Log Off' button if they do not intend coming back to work at the PC as this frees up the memory required to store their Desktop and open programs.

Bright idea
To make your My Documents folder private so other users cannot access it, right-click on it, choose Properties and select the Sharing tab. Put a tick next to 'Make this folder private'.

Key word
If you have to log on to a computer to use it, you need to prove you are authorised to do so – usually by clicking on a user icon and typing a password. When you log off, you're telling the computer that you intend to stop using it for the time being.

Accessibility programs

If you have a sight, hearing or mobility impairment, Windows has lots of options to make operating your PC easier. It's possible to use your keyboard to operate the mouse pointer and buttons, and you can instruct Windows to replace warning sounds with on-screen displays. You can also use an on-screen keyboard and even have Windows read out text or magnify it.

ACCESSIBILITY PROGRAMS

You can access these tools by clicking on the Start button, All Programs, Accessories and Accessibility.

Magnify your screen

The Magnifier program is designed to help people with impaired vision. When you run Magnifier, the top section of your screen becomes an enlarged view of your working area.

It tracks what you're doing by displaying the mouse pointer or any text you're typing. To launch Magnifier, click on **Accessibility** and then **Magnifier**. In the Magnifier Settings dialogue box, you can choose the level of magnification and change the screen colours, if this helps.

Use an on-screen keyboard

If you find the mouse easier to use than the keyboard, try the on-screen keyboard instead. Click on **Accessibility** and choose **On-Screen Keyboard**. To type, click the keys you require with your mouse. You can customise the way the keyboard works via its Settings menu.

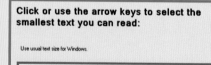

Let the wizard do it for you

The Accessibility Wizard is an easy way to adapt your PC. Launch the Accessibility Wizard from the **Accessibility** menu. The wizard's dialogue box appears and asks a series of questions to ascertain your sight, hearing and mobility needs. Follow the instructions and, when you're ready, click on **Finish**. If you're not happy with the settings, you can run the Wizard again, or try adjusting each setting using the Accessibility Options dialogue box, which is accessed via Control Panel (see opposite).

> **Click or use the arrow keys to select the smallest text you can read:**
>
> Use usual text size for Windows.
>
> Use large window titles and menus.
>
> **Use Microsoft Magnifier, and large titles and menus.**

Expert advice
To move the cursor with MouseKeys use the numeric keypad on your keyboard: up = **8**, down = **2**, left = **4**, and right = **6**. To move diagonally, press either the **7**, **9**, **1** or **3** keys. To click, press **5**. To double-click, press the **+** (plus) key. To right-click press the **-** (minus) key followed by **5**. The '5' key will continue to act as a right-click until you press **/** to switch back to normal clicking.

Close up
If you need to make the magnified area bigger, place your cursor on the line between the normal screen and the magnified section. When the double-headed arrow appears, just click and drag to increase the area.

SIGHT, SOUND AND TOUCH

Set up your keyboard and display to suit you, thus making your PC as comfortable as possible to use.

Adjust your keyboard

If you find typing difficult, Windows has settings to make the keyboard easier to use. Click on the **Start** menu and select **Control Panel**. Click on the **Accessibility Options** icon and then on **Accessibility Options**. In the Accessibility Options dialogue box, select the **Keyboard** tab. There are several options available. If you have difficulty holding down the Shift, Ctrl or Alt keys with another key when you carry out a keyboard command, place a tick next to ' Use StickyKeys'.

Click on the **Settings** button under 'StickyKeys' and, in the 'Options' section, put a tick next to 'Press modifier key twice to lock'. Next time you want to use a keyboard command, simply press the **Ctrl**, **Shift** or **Alt** key twice to avoid holding them down. If you tend to press keys more than once accidentally, put a tick next to 'Use FilterKeys'. This instructs Windows to ignore brief repeated keystrokes. The final option is 'Use ToggleKeys'. This makes a sound if you press the Caps Lock, Num Lock or Scroll Lock keys, which is handy if you hit these keys by accident.

Visual alerts

Select the **Sound** tab. SoundSentry gives you a visual warning whenever your system makes an alert sound. Click on the down arrow to the right of the 'Choose the visual warning' box to select what kind of signal you get, such as your Desktop flashing. If you would like to see a caption when your PC makes a sound, tick the 'Use ShowSounds' box instead of SoundSentry.

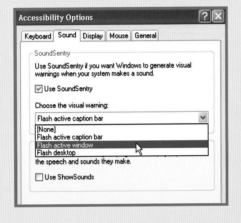

Easy viewing

If you have poor eyesight, you can make the screen easier to read. Click the **Display** tab in the Accessibility Options dialogue box. If you choose 'Use High Contrast', your monitor will use contrasting colours, such as white on a black background, and large fonts. Click **Settings** to choose a colour combination. Under 'Cursor Options' adjust the rate at which the cursor blinks and the thickness of your cursor.

Keyboard mouse control

If you find the keyboard easier to use than the mouse, try MouseKeys. In the Accessibility Options dialogue box, select the **Mouse** tab. Tick the 'Use MouseKeys' box. You can now use the numeric keypad to control the movement of your mouse pointer and its button actions. To swap between using the keys as numbers and as MouseKeys, simply press the **Num Lock** key.

Narrator

If you have vision impairments, Narrator can help by reading out the contents of the active window, text you have typed or menu options. You can launch Narrator from the Accessibility menu – it will appear as a button on the Taskbar.

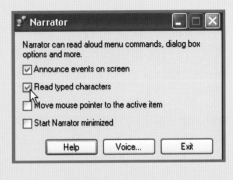

Click on the Taskbar button to see the options. You can have Narrator read out new windows and menus as soon as they are displayed and even read out text and numbers as you type them in. Hold down the **Ctrl** and **Shift** keys and press the **Spacebar** to have Narrator repeat any text. To start Narrator quickly, hold down the **Windows** key and press **U**. This also opens the Windows Utility Manager.

Utility Manager

You can configure accessibility programs to start automatically when you log in to Windows or when you press the 'Windows' and 'U' keys. Open the Utility Manager, select the utility you want to configure (such as Magnifier) and put ticks next to the actions to be performed. Click the **Start** button to start a utility immediately and the **Stop** button to close it down.

Create your own shortcuts

Once you have an understanding of Windows and its programs, you can create 'shortcuts' to help you work more quickly. A shortcut is an icon on your Desktop or Taskbar, or an entry on your Start menu, which is linked to a program, file or folder. The shortcut launches the related item immediately, which saves you searching through multiple menus or folders.

QUICK LINKS

Create shortcuts to folders, documents and programs for quick and easy access.

Extra programs in the Start menu

You can add a program to the top of the Start menu simply by dragging the program icon onto it from its location under All Programs. Locate the item to which you want to add a shortcut, click on it and hold down the left button while you drag it to a new position above the grey line in the Start menu. Let go and the shortcut will appear.

Program shortcuts on your Desktop

To make a shortcut to a program, right-click anywhere on the **Desktop**, select **New** and click on **Shortcut**.
In the Create Shortcut dialogue box click on the **Browse** button. Locate the

relevant program in the Browse For Folder dialogue box by clicking on the folders and drives under 'Select the target of the shortcut below'. Scroll down and click on relevant folders to open them. Select the program, click on **OK** and click the **Next** button. Choose a name and click on the **Finish** button. The shortcut, which looks like the program icon with a small arrow, appears on your Desktop.

Paint Shop Pro 6

Desktop documents

You can also create Desktop shortcuts for documents that you use regularly. Locate the file in its folder and right-click on it. Click on **Send To** on the pop-up menu and then choose **Desktop (create shortcut)**. A shortcut icon appears on the Desktop. Drag and drop the shortcut wherever you like on the Desktop.

An alternative method is to drag the item to your **Desktop** while holding down the right mouse button instead of the left button. When you let go, a pop-up menu appears. Choose **Create Shortcuts Here** to put the shortcut on your Desktop. Now, to open the document, just double-click on the shortcut icon.

Copy Here
Move Here
Create Shortcuts Here
Cancel

Shortcut to My Work

The ultimate time-saver

Set up a program so it launches when you start your PC. Click on the **Start** button and choose **My Computer**. In the right-hand pane,

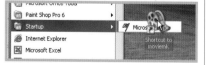

find the program on the hard disk. Drag the program over your **Start** button without letting go. Hover the mouse there and the Start menu will open. Then hover the icon over **All Programs**. When the submenu opens, drag to **Startup** and then to its submenu. This puts a shortcut into the Startup folder.

Close up

To remove a program shortcut, click on it and drag it onto the Recycle Bin. This won't delete the program itself, which is still in the Program Files folder, because the shortcut is just a link to it.

Windows' Built-in Programs

Using WordPad and Notepad

Windows comes with a basic word processor called WordPad. Despite its simplicity, this program can be used to create documents containing a mixture of formats and graphics. Windows also includes Notepad. This is a very simple text editor, which is useful for creating documents, such as Web pages, where hidden text formatting codes might cause problems.

Key word
A font is a specific style and set of characters within a typeface, for example 'Arial Bold Italic' or 'Times New Roman'.

BEFORE YOU START
*Click on the **Start** button and select **All Programs**. Then click on Accessories and scroll down to WordPad to open it. A blank document will appear.*

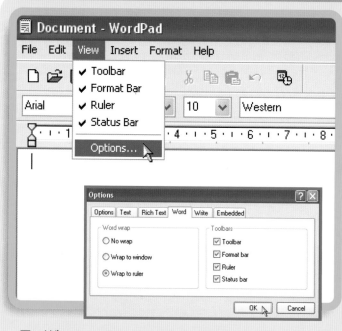

1 When you open WordPad, you will see a blank page with a flashing cursor at the top. This is called the 'insertion point' – the place on screen where the text appears when you begin typing. Click on the **View** menu, choose **Options** and click on the **Word** tab. Then put a dot next to 'Wrap to ruler' and click on **OK**.

2 When you've typed in some text, try styling it. Select the text and click on the buttons on the Format Bar: the **B** stands for bold, the **I** stands for italic, the **U** stands for underline and the **Palette** enables you to choose a text colour. Next to these are the alignment buttons. You can align your text to the left, the right or the centre. Click on the **Format** menu to see more styling options.

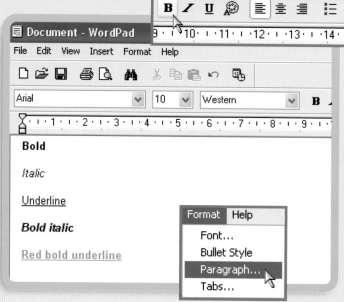

50

Bright idea
To select a word, click just before or just after it and hold down your left mouse button whilst dragging across it. Quicker still, just double-click on top of the word you want to select. Clicking three times in quick succession in WordPad highlights the whole paragraph.

Notepad
Launch Notepad by clicking on the **Start** button, followed by **All Programs**, **Accessories** and then **Notepad**. To change the font and text size, click on the **Format** menu and choose **Font** – Notepad will retain these settings until you change them again. Select **WordWrap** to fit the text into the width of the window. If you want to apply formatting, such as colours or underline, you cannot do this in Notepad, so copy your text into WordPad. Select all the text, click on the **Edit** menu and choose **Copy**. Then open **WordPad**, click on its **Edit** menu and select **Paste**.

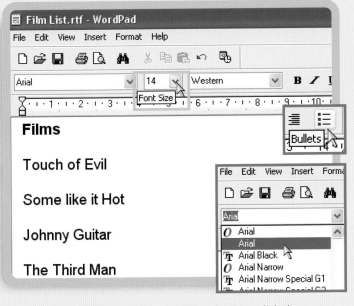

4 To save your page, click on the **File** menu then **Save**. Choose a location for your file in the 'Save in' box. Then type a name in the 'File name' box. Choose a file format in the 'Save as type' panel: to keep the formatting you have applied, choose **Rich Text Format** (Word can open rich text documents). For a plain text file, which will have no formatting, choose **Text document**. Finally, click on **Save**. To print your page, click on the **File** menu and select **Print**. Then click on **Print**.

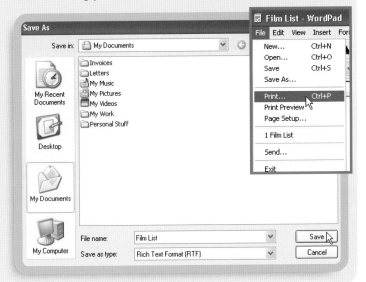

3 Now type a list, pressing the **Return** key after each item. Highlight the list and click on the **Bullets** button, or go to the **Format** menu and choose **Bullet Style**. To change font, select the text, click the arrow next to the font name and scroll through the drop-down list to select another font. You can also change the font size in the drop-down menu to the right of the font list.

Address Book

Create a comprehensive directory of everyone you know with the Address Book, which can hold names, addresses and information such as birthdays. You can access the Address Book directly, or through Outlook Express (which is included with Windows XP) or via third party Personal Information Managers (PIMs).

Watch out
If you have contact details stored in Microsoft Outlook, you will first need to export them as a separate document from Outlook into your My Documents folder, and then you can import them from there into the Address Book.

BEFORE YOU START
Make sure all your contacts' details are correct. To open the Address Book, go to the **Start** menu, **All Programs**, **Accessories** then **Address Book**.

1 In the left pane of the Address Book window are two folders: Shared Contacts and Main Identity's Contacts. These folders are handy if more than one person uses the PC (see page 44). Use the Main Identity's Contacts folder for contact details that are personal to you. Use the Shared Contacts folder for contacts to which everyone using the PC needs access.

2 To create a new entry, click on the folder in which you wish the details to be held. Then click on the **File** menu and select **New Contact**. Enter the contact's name under the 'Name' tab. Fill in the 'E-Mail Addresses' panel and click on **Add**. You can input as many e-mail addresses as you need. Select the address your contact uses most often and click on **Set as Default**.

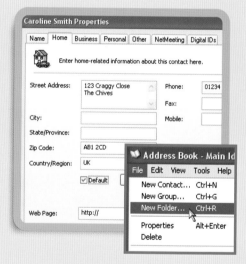

3 To the right of the 'Name' tab are six tabs. Use these to add details such as a contact's work address, home address and birthday. When you've finished, click on **OK**. You can create separate folders for work contacts, relatives and so on. Click on the **File** menu, select **New Folder** and choose a name. To reorganise your contacts, click and drag them into the other folders.

Expert advice
To delete a contact from your Address Book, click on the relevant name, press the **Delete** key and then click on **Yes**. Be careful – this deleted information does not go into the Recycle Bin so these details cannot be recovered later.

Bright idea
To send an e-mail to a contact in your Address Book, right-click on their name, select Action *and then* Send Mail. *A New Message window will open in your e-mail program with the contact's e-mail address already in the 'To' panel.*

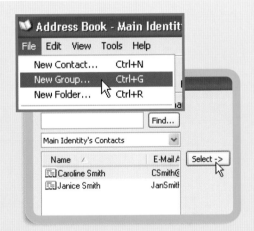

5 As your list of contacts grows, you will need to be able to find the one you want quickly and easily. One way of doing this is to click the **Find People** button on the toolbar. Type in the name of your contact, or any part of it, and then click on **Find Now**. Alternatively, you can search using other criteria by clicking on the **View** menu, selecting **Sort By** and then selecting the criteria.

4 If you often send e-mails to several people at once – for instance, members of a club – you can collect their addresses in a Group. To create a new group, click on the **File** menu then select **New Group**. Give your new group a name and click **Select Members**. Choose each person, clicking **Select** each time, then click on **OK**. Every time you wish to e-mail those people, just type the group name in the 'To' panel of your new e-mail message.

6 You can import another e-mail program's contacts into the Address Book or export your details to a different program. Click on the **File** menu and select **Import** or **Export**. Then select **Other Address Book**. The Import option covers many common e-mail programs – select one and click on **Import**. To export, choose **Text File** and click on the **Export** button. Select the 'Address Book (WAB)' option to make a backup of your Address Book.

Movie Maker

The latest video camera technology lets you record your movies digitally and then transfer them directly to your PC. Using the Movie Maker program supplied with Windows, you can edit those movies and then share them by saving them onto a recordable CD, posting them on your Web site, or by sending them anywhere in the world by e-mail.

Close up
When Movie Maker creates clips, these are only references to your videos – the actual files remain in their original locations on your hard disk so make sure you don't move or delete them.

BEFORE YOU START
You may need to install software for your camcorder on your PC.

Check the manual for details on how to transfer your movie clips from the camera to your PC.

1 Click on the **Start** button and select **All Programs**, then **Accessories** and **Windows Movie Maker**. Once you have copied your video across to your PC, click on **Import video** in the Movie Tasks pane and browse to the folder in which you stored your videos. Select a file and click on **Import**. Movie Maker converts your video to 'Clips', which it places in the Collection pane. You can play a clip by selecting it and clicking on the **Play** button (see right) in the Monitor pane.

2 Along the bottom of the window is the 'Storyboard'. To insert the clips in your movie, drag them from the Collection pane and drop them in the large squares on the Storyboard, starting at the left. To preview your movie, click on the first clip on the Storyboard, then click on the **Play** button in the Monitor pane.

3 If you want to split a clip, for example, if you want to delete a section, select the clip in the Collection pane and move the playback indicator to the point at which you want to split it. Then click on the **Clip** menu and choose **Split**. Your clip now divides into two separate clips. Drag the one you want to use to the Storyboard and leave the one you don't want to use. Change the order of the clips on the Storyboard by dragging them. A vertical blue line shows the position the clip will occupy as soon as you let go of the button.

E-mailing your movie

If you want to e-mail your movie, select **Send in e-mail** under 'Finish Movie' (see step 6). Movie Maker creates your movie – this may take a little while depending on how long it is. When it has finished, you are given the option to play the movie to check it one more time, or to save it before you send it. Click on **Next** when you are finished. Movie Maker opens your e-mail program and creates a new message with the movie attached.

Watch out

Not all PCs have the connector that a camcorder requires in order to 'talk' to your PC. Modern digital video cameras use a special high-speed link, which requires an IEEE 1394 (FireWire) port on your PC. You may need to purchase an IEEE 1394 adaptor in order to copy your movies to your PC.

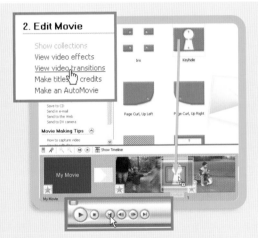

5 You can add titles and credits to your movie too. Click on **Make titles or credits** under 'Edit Movie' in the Movie Tasks pane and choose from the list of options. Type in your text – you can preview it in the Monitor pane as you type – and click on **Done, add title to movie** when you've finished. Then click on the **Back** and **Play** buttons to preview the movie.

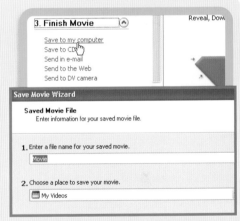

4 Movie Maker comes with built-in 'transitions'. These are animated effects that play between video clips. As one clip comes to an end, the transition takes you smoothly, using the selected effect, to the beginning of the next clip. To insert a transition, click on **Edit Movie** in the Movie Tasks pane, and then click on **View video transitions**. Click and drag a transition to the squares between the clips on the Storyboard. Click on **Back** and then **Play**.

6 Once you have all the clips and transitions in the right order (see step 3), save your movie by choosing one of the options under 'Finish Movie' in the Movie Tasks pane. This launches the Save Movie Wizard, which provides step-by-step guidance to help you save your movie in the right format. For instance, if you choose 'Save to my computer', all you need to do is to choose a name and location for your movie and Movie Maker does the rest.

Media Player

Windows' Media Player is a multimedia program supplied with Windows that allows you to play many audio and video formats. Audio sources include CDs, Internet radio stations and sound files you've downloaded from the Internet or created from a CD. You can also watch video files from CDs and DVDs, or log on to the Internet and view news footage.

GETTING STARTED

Click on the Start menu and select All Programs, then Accessories, Entertainment, and Windows Media Player. Media Player also appears as an icon on the Quick Launch toolbar.

Getting started

Media Player is an extremely versatile entertainment program, capable of playing back most types of audio and video file. You can control all the playing options from the Media

Player window – the buttons down the left-hand side list the main features, and the buttons along the bottom control your listening and viewing settings.

Visualizations

While you are listening to music, you can watch colourful patterns, called 'Visualizations', which respond to the type of music you are playing. There are around 75 styles to choose from, organised in categories. Click on the **View** menu, select **Visualizations** and click a sub-menu. Click on any option to see it in the window (make sure you have some music playing), or click on the left and right arrows beneath the Visualization window to scroll through the choices. You must click on the **Now Playing** button when you are playing music to see a selected Visualization in action.

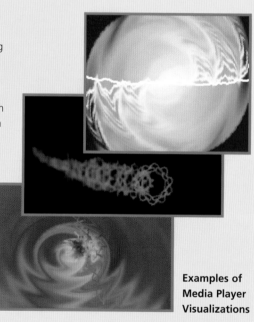

Examples of Media Player Visualizations

Close up
You can view Media Player in Full Screen mode. To do this, select this option from the View *menu, or click the button with the diagonal arrow at the bottom right of the Visualization window.*

THE MEDIA PLAYER WINDOW

This window gives you all the control options you need for the various Media Player features, together with a central viewing area.

Playlist chooser

AutoHide menu bar displays or hides the menu.

Now Playing shows you what files are currently in use, for example, which CD is playing and the duration of each track.

Media Guide links to the WindowsMedia.com Web site where you can download the latest news footage.

Copy from CD lets you copy CD tracks onto your hard disk and file them in the My Music folder.

Media Library allows you to organise all the media files on your PC.

Radio Tuner lets you listen to Internet radio stations around the world.

Copy to CD or Device allows you to transfer music files from your PC to a device such as an MP3 player.

Premium Services offers a range of subscription services, including movies on demand.

Skin Chooser changes the appearance of the Media Player by applying a graphical colour scheme known as a 'skin'.

Play/ Pause

Stop

Previous track

Next track

Volume adjust
Mute sound

Seek indicator

Previous/Next Visualization lets you select an animated pattern to accompany your sound files.

Switch to Skin
Change colour

Bright idea
When you right-click on a selected CD track you get several useful options, which allow you to rate the track, to delete it from the playlist or to view its properties. You can also select the order in which you want the tracks to play.

Close up
Click on the Skin Chooser button to select from a list of colour schemes and interface styles. If you can't find one you like, connect to the Internet and click on the More Skins button. This takes you to a Microsoft Web site where you can download featured skins.

That's amazing!
Media Player can copy tracks from a
CD and save them as files on your hard
drive so you can listen to them without
inserting the disc. These are called **WMA**
files. Insert a CD and click on **Copy from
CD** on the left of the Media Player window. Deselect the
tracks you don't want and click on **Copy Music**.

Key word
*WMA stands for Windows Media
Audio. WMA files are compressed
files, which take up much less space
than the original CD audio files. However, the
sound quality is not compromised, thanks to
smart technology that compresses the data
before it is recorded to hard disk.*

PLAYING AN AUDIO CD

1 When you insert a music CD in
your CD drive, Windows will ask
you what action to take. If you
want Media Player to launch every time
you insert an audio CD, put a tick next to
'Always do the selected action' and click
on **OK**. Otherwise, select **Play audio CD**
from the list under 'What do you want
Windows to do?' and click on **OK**.

2 Media Player will begin playing
the first track on the CD. If you
are connected to the Internet, it
will also download an image of the
album cover and all the track names
automatically. You can select any track
by double-clicking its name.

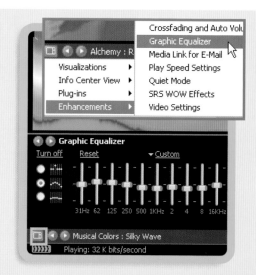

3 To adjust the bass or treble
settings, click on the **Select
Now Playing options** button,
choose **Enhancements** and select
Graphic Equalizer. The sliders fine tune
the bass and treble, from left to right.
Simply click and drag each vertical slider
until you get the tone you want. Or you
can choose a preset equaliser setting
from the list under 'Custom'.

Bright idea
To adjust the volume level of Media Player, you don't need to change the overall Windows volume. Simply drag the Media Player volume slider (see page 57) to the right to increase, or to the left to decrease, the sound level.

Watch out
The sound quality of your copied audio tracks depends on the setting at which they are copied. More Kbps (kilobits per second) means the file takes up more disk space but is better quality. Less Kbps results in a smaller file but with poorer sound quality. To alter this setting, click on the **Tools** menu, select **Options**, then click the **Copy Music** tab.

LISTEN TO ONLINE RADIO

1 To tune in to an Internet radio station, first connect to the Internet then click on the **Radio Tuner** button on the left of the Media Player window. In the panel on the right, you can choose from featured stations or use the preset categories to locate a station. If you know the name (or part of the name) of a station, type it in the Search box and click the green arrow button to the right. Media Player displays a list of stations matching your search.

2 Click on a station and a panel will open up displaying options: you can add the selected station to your My Stations list, listen to it by visiting the broadcaster's Web site or listen to it directly through Media Player. Click on the **Play** button to start listening. If a Security Warning box appears, click on the **Yes** button.

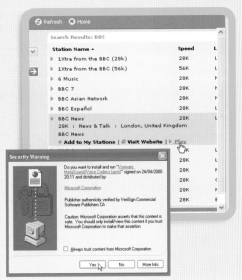

3 Click the **Home** button to return to the Radio Tuner screen at any time. From here, you can click on the **My Stations** link to see the list of stations you have added. Click on the double downward arrow button next to a station to show more information. To remove the station from the list, click on the **Remove from My Stations** link.

Paint

Windows' built-in Paint program is perfect for creating simple yet colourful graphics. You can use it to sketch diagrams such as maps, or to create a new pattern for your Desktop background. You might even want to design a logo or make a picture for a card. All the pictures created in Paint can be saved for use in other Windows programs.

SEE ALSO...

● *Personalise your Desktop* p 40

HOW IT WORKS

Paint is perfect for making small posters, leaflets, invitations and cards.

Open Paint by clicking on the **Start** button, **All Programs**, **Accessories**, then **Paint**. The File and Edit headings on the Menu bar contain commands that allow you to open and save files, and cut and paste items as you would in a Word document. To change the size of the painting area, called the 'canvas', click on the **Image** menu and select **Attributes**.

The Tool Box
A panel on the left contains 16 tools. Hover the pointer over each to see its name.

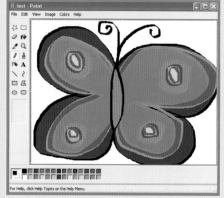

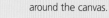

Free-Form Select Allows you to select an irregularly shaped area. Click and drag as if you are drawing freehand to define the selection area.

Select Click and drag a rectangular box over an item to select it. You can then click and drag the item to move it around the canvas.

Eraser Rubs out unwanted elements of an image. Alter the eraser size using the blocks under the tool palette.

Fill With Color Fills a selected area with the foreground colour of your choice from the colour palette.

Pick Color Click on a colour in your image to copy it to the colour palette, for use with another tool.

Magnifier Zooms in on the image. Choose a magnification level from the list below the tool palette.

Pencil Allows you to draw thin freehand lines. Click and drag to draw.

Brush Draws like the pencil but with 12 different style options that appear below the Tool Box.

Airbrush Creates the illusion of sprayed paint across your image in a choice of three widths.

Text Adds words to the picture. Click where you want to begin, drag to create a text box, and type.

Expert advice
Paint can open and save 'Bitmap', 'jpeg', 'gif', 'tiff' and 'png' files: **bitmap** is perfect for photographs saved on your PC; **jpeg** is a compressed format, used for photos on Web sites and digital cameras; **gifs** can only include up to 256 colours and are used for buttons and animations on Web sites; **tiffs** are best suited to photographs; and **png** was designed to replace the 'gif' format.

Close up
If you want to reposition the Tool Box, click on any part of it that does not contain a button and drag it to another location. To return it to its original location, click and drag it to the left side of the window and it will snap back into place.

Bright idea
Hold down the Shift *key while you drag out a rectangle shape to draw a perfect square. This also applies when you drag an ellipse to create a circle.*

Line Draws straight lines of the width you choose from the panel below the Tool Box.

Curve Draws curves of a chosen width. Click to define a start point and drag to define an end point. Click on the line and drag to bend it into a curve.

Rectangle Draw a rectangle, choosing from: an outline only, a filled rectangle with an outline, or a solid rectangle.

Polygon Draws a many-sided figure. Click and drag for the first side, then click on subsequent points and the lines are drawn automatically.

Ellipse Click and drag to create a circle or oval using same style options as the rectangle (above).

Rounded rectangle This lets you draw a shape similar to a rectangle but with rounded corners.

Colours

The Color Box contains 28 coloured squares. The two overlapping squares on the left of the box indicate foreground (drawing) and background colour.

To change the drawing colour, click on a colour. To change the background, right-click on a colour.

Double-click on a colour to open the Edit Colors dialogue box. To customise the palette, click on **Define Custom Colors**. Click on a new colour in the Color Matrix and adjust the lightness with the slider on the right, then click on **Add to Custom Colors**. You can choose up to 16 custom colours to replace the preset colours. Then click on **OK**.

Saving a image

Click on the **File** menu and select **Save**. Windows saves Paint files to the My Pictures folder by default. Name your file and choose a format by clicking the down arrow to the right of 'Save as type'. The best format for saving images is '24-bit Bitmap'. But if you want to save space on your hard drive, choose 'jpeg' as the file is compressed while retaining most of its quality.

Wallpaper

You can use any image you have drawn, or one to which you have added colours or text, as the background of your Desktop. In Paint, go to the **File** menu and select **Set As Background**. Selecting the 'Tiled' option means the image will repeat across your screen (see right), while 'Centred' will position the image in the middle of your screen.

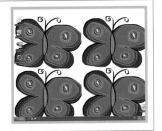

Close up
To change an image on the Windows Desktop background, right-click on the Desktop *and select* Properties*. In the Display Properties dialogue box, click on the* Desktop *tab and select another picture or* None *from the list under Background. Click* OK*.*

Calculator

Sometimes, when working on a document or writing an e-mail, you might need the help of a calculator. To save you scrambling through your desk drawers to find one, Windows includes an on-screen version. It works in the same way as an ordinary calculator, but you use either the numeric keypad on your keyboard or the mouse to click the buttons.

SEE ALSO...
- *Create your own shortcuts* p 48
- *Using WordPad and Notepad* p 50

STANDARD CALCULATOR

To access the Calculator, click on the Start button and select All Programs, Accessories and then Calculator.

The Windows Calculator works in the same way as a normal one but some of the button symbols are different. The '/' symbol, for example, is for division and '*' for multiplication.

Numeric keypad and keyboard

All the buttons have a keyboard equivalent. The numbers and the plus, minus, multiply and divide buttons are on the numeric pad to the far right of your keyboard. Press **Enter** for equals (=), **Delete** to clear the screen ('CE' in the calculator) and the **Esc** key to clear the calculation. When you use the number keypad, make sure a green light is showing next to 'Num Lock'. If not, press **Num Lock** on the keyboard to activate it.

Buttons on the left are for memory options.

M appears in this box when a number is stored in the memory.

MC clears the calculator's memory.

MR recalls a stored figure (only one can be stored at any time).

MS stores a figure in the memory.

M+ adds the figure in the display to the figure in the memory.

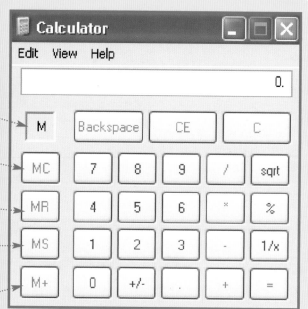

Expert advice

If you use the Calculator often, add a shortcut to the Desktop. Click on the **Start** button, select **All Programs** and **Accessories** and right-click on **Calculator**. Choose **Send To** from the pop-up list and then select **Desktop (create shortcut)**. A new shortcut appears on your Desktop – click on it and drag it to reposition it.

You can use the Standard Calculator to work out percentages. For example, to add VAT at 17.5 per cent to £150, click on the buttons to enter '150+17.5', click on the **%** button and then on the **=** button. Or you could subtract VAT from an inclusive amount using the keyboard. For example, type in '£65.50-17.5%' and press the **Enter** key.

If you are unsure about the function of any of the buttons on the Standard or Scientific Calculators, right-click on the button about which you want information and choose **What's This?**. A pop-up box appears, with a brief description of the button and its keyboard equivalent.

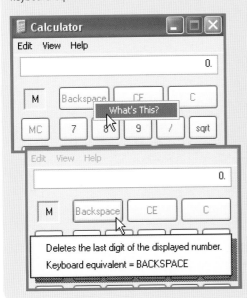

Scientific Calculator

To access a more sophisticated calculator (below), click on the **View** menu and select **Scientific**. You can work in different number base systems. We normally use decimals (Base 10), but binary, octal and hexadecimal systems (2, 8 and 16) are available. If trigonometry is your speciality, select the options at the top of the calculator for working in Degrees, Radians and Grads. There are also Inverse and Hyperbolic options. If you need to perform advanced statistical calculations, press the blue **Sta** button on the left to activate the grey buttons below it.

Digit grouping

Both the Standard and Scientific Calculators can display up to 32 digits. Add commas as thousand separators by clicking on the **View** menu and putting a tick next to 'Digit grouping'. Even with commas, the Calculator displays up to 32 digits.

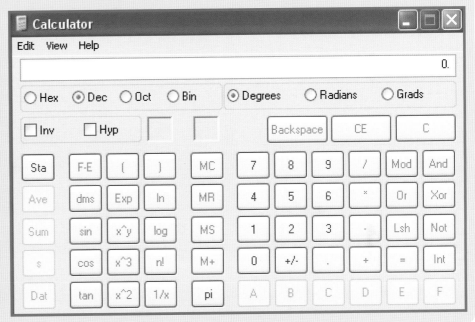

Close up
Be sure to click the C button or press the Esc key on your keyboard between each calculation. This will clear the calculator screen and ensure that your answer doesn't become cumulative.

63

Games

Windows XP comes with a selection of games, ranging from the fun and easy-to-play Pinball, to more challenging card games such as Hearts and the compulsive FreeCell. None of these games require special features on your PC, but if you are connected to the Internet there are another five games that let you play against other people online.

EXPLORE THE GAMES
From the Start menu select All Programs, followed by Games. Then select the game you want to play.

Hearts
Click on **Hearts**, type your name in the panel and click **OK**. Hearts is a game of simple strategy, played in rounds until one player reaches a score of 100, at which point the player with the lowest score wins the game.

At the beginning of the first round, each player chooses three cards to pass to the opponent on their left – it's a good idea to pass high scoring cards (kings, queens and aces) and high hearts, because you don't want to win too many tricks. Simply click on the three you want to pass on and then click on the **Pass** button. On the next round, the three cards are passed to the right and on the third round, to the

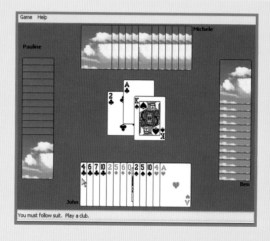

player opposite. On the fourth round, no cards are passed. This continues throughout the game and Windows sets this up automatically for you. When each player has passed three cards, the player holding the two of clubs begins the first

hand by playing it. Each player, moving clockwise, must play a card of the same suit if he or she has one. Otherwise any card can be played (note that on the first trick you cannot play a heart or the queen of spades).

The trick of four cards is won by the player who plays the highest card of the same suit as the first card played. You should try to avoid winning tricks, especially early in the game.

At the end of a round, all the cards in the tricks you have won are added up – you get one point for each heart, and 13 points for the queen of spades. If a player collects all the hearts and the queen of spades, this is called 'Shooting the Moon' and everyone else gets 26 points while they get none.

Remember who has scored the most points – if you are not the player with the least points, you risk losing if you force that player to win a scoring trick and go over 100 points.

That's amazing!
If you are playing on a networked PC, you can have up to four people playing the same game of Hearts at the same time. And if there are only two or three of you, the computer will simulate the other players.

Bright idea
Use 'ducking' to avoid winning tricks. This is where you play the highest card you have that is lower than the highest card played by the others. Watch out though, as you could end up with high cards near the end of a round.

Solitaire

The object of Solitaire is to end up with four suit stacks of cards at the top right of the screen in ascending suit order (beginning with the aces).

At the start of play, there are seven stacks of cards in a row – the first holds one card, the last holds seven. The top cards are face up. If any are aces, you can use the mouse to move them to the four stacks at the top right of the screen

immediately. You must build the seven stacks by dragging a card to another card of the opposite colour and one higher position in the suit – for example, the jack of clubs can be placed on the queen of hearts, or the seven of diamonds can be placed on the eight of spades. You can also drag across a sequence of cards. If you can't move any cards from other stacks, click on the deck at the top left to draw new cards, and drag them to the stacks where possible.

As aces come up, double-click on them to place them on the stacks at the right. Start to build up the suit stacks by dragging the cards around. If a column is empty, you can either drag a king there from the deck or drag a

sequence of cards starting with a king from another stack. Then turn over a new card in the stack, if there's one left.

Under the 'Game' menu there are several options: **Deal** starts a new game; **Options** allows you to choose whether cards are dealt in groups of three, or one at a time; and **Deck** enables you to change the pattern of your deck by selecting one of the options.

FreeCell

Click on the **Game** menu in the FreeCell window and select **New Game**. Click on **Select Game** to choose a specific game numbered between 1 and 1,000,000. In theory, every game can be won, but you can go back to restart a game which has beaten you.

FreeCell differs from most Solitaire games because all the cards are visible right from the start. The object is similar to Solitaire, which is to get all of the cards into the Home cells at the top right of the screen, in the same suits, ascending from the ace. Move cards by clicking on them, and then clicking where you want them to go. You can only move a card to another column when it is one card lower than its destination card in rank or number and is the opposite colour – sequences of cards can also be moved. There are four cells at the top left where cards can be temporarily placed and brought back into play later. When a column is empty, you can move other cards onto it. If you are not sure what card is beneath another, right-click on the visible portion to reveal it.

Bright idea
If you want to play a game without anyone else knowing, open another program, such as Word or Excel, and use the Minimize button to reduce it to an icon on the Taskbar. While playing the game, a quick click will restore the work window, hiding your game.

Minesweeper

When the game opens you will see a pad with a grid of grey squares. A number of bombs are hidden beneath the squares. Click on the **Game** menu to choose your level – this alters the size of the grid and the number of bombs.

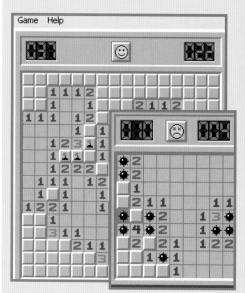

The timer starts when you click on your first square. Click on any square in the grid. It will either disappear, taking lots of adjoining empty squares with it and displaying numbers on those around the edges, or show a bomb and explode (meaning that you've lost the game).

Numbered squares tell you how many bombs are in the eight squares surrounding the one you have selected. Using skill and logic, you can deduce where the bombs are hidden. Right-click to put a warning flag on a square you think is hiding a bomb. Right-click twice to place an 'unsure' question mark instead.

Pinball

This looks like a classic Pinball machine and, like the real thing, you fire a ball and catapult it round the machine, trying to hit the point scoring elements. When the ball drops between the flippers, you can no longer score and the next ball becomes available. There are three balls to a game. Once it has loaded, press **F2** on your keyboard for a new game. Draw back the rod by holding down the **Spacebar**, and release it to fire the ball. Deflect the ball around the machine using **Z** for the left flipper and **/** for the right. If the pinball gets stuck, press **Full**

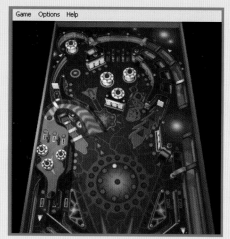

stop (.), the **Up** arrow key, or **X** to nudge the machine. To alter these elements click on the **Options** menu and select **Player Controls**. At the end of the game, a dialogue box shows the score. Click **OK** to exit the box.

Spider Solitaire

If you want a better chance of winning a card game, Spider Solitaire is for you. The object is to clear the board of cards by stacking them from king to ace in the left-hand corner of the board, but this time there are ten columns. The only criteria is that the cards must be stacked in

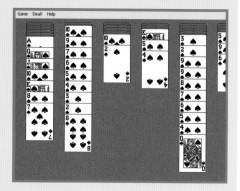

descending order. Once the game has loaded, a Difficulty dialogue box appears on screen offering different levels. In the easiest level, all cards are the same suit, while in the most difficult level there are four suits. You can place any colour card on another one, but you cannot move a column of cards unless they are all of the same suit.

Watch out

If you want to play 3-D games, check that your PC's specifications match the game's recommended minimum requirements. These will be printed on the side of the box. The main considerations are the amount of RAM in your PC and how powerful your graphics card is.

The scoring system means that you start with 500 points and lose a point every time you move a card or undo a move. You gain 100 points for each king to ace stack you complete. Try to free up cards from the top of stacks to keep cards in suits for added flexibility. If you are stuck for a move, press **M** and the computer suggests one.

Internet games

There are five games on your computer which you can play on the Internet. Return to the **Games** menu and select one of the Internet games from the sub-menu.

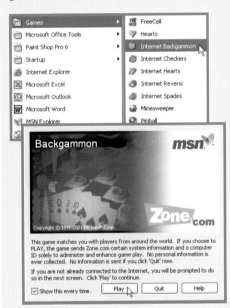

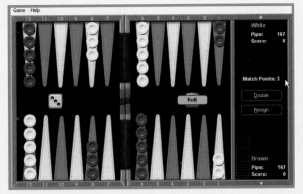

Click on **Play** in the open program window. You are taken to the Microsoft Game Center and will be connected to another player sitting at their computer somewhere else in the world, and waiting to play. You can choose to chat or to remain silent by selecting the appropriate

radio button. If you have chosen a dice game, just click on the dice to start playing.

Backgammon, Reversi and Checkers are designed for two online players, whilst the card games can be played by up to four online players at once.

Other games

There are many other games that you can play, but they have to be purchased. Some are games of skill or logic, others use your PC's power to create virtual 3-D worlds, in which you can pilot a jet plane, play a round of golf on a famous course, race in a Formula 1 Grand Prix or seek treasure in lost tombs with explorers.

Generally, games only take up a moderate amount of disk space, but you may need to keep the game's CD in the drive while you play. Most have an auto-install feature to guide you through their setup before you first play them. The more powerful your computer and its graphics card, the faster and more realistic the games will be.

Peripheral control devices can be added to increase the fun or realism of games, for example a steering wheel and pedals for driving games, or a joystick for flight simulators and shooting games.

Many gaming sites on the Internet allow you to play against other people, although you may have to download an extra piece of software to do so.

That's amazing!
The Microsoft Games Center (www.zone.com) enables you to play online against other people of similar ability from all over the world. The Games Center will even let you send selected messages to your opponents in their language, such as 'your move' or 'bad luck'.

Windows Messenger

The ability to communicate electronically via the Internet is integral to Windows XP, and Messenger plays a key role in providing this. With this program you can chat and instantly swap files with contacts, and even conduct video conferences or telephone calls. It's easy to set up so you'll soon be chatting to relatives and friends anywhere, at any time.

BEFORE YOU START
If you don't have an Internet connection, open Help and Support (see page 86), search for 'Internet Connection Wizard' and follow the suggested steps.

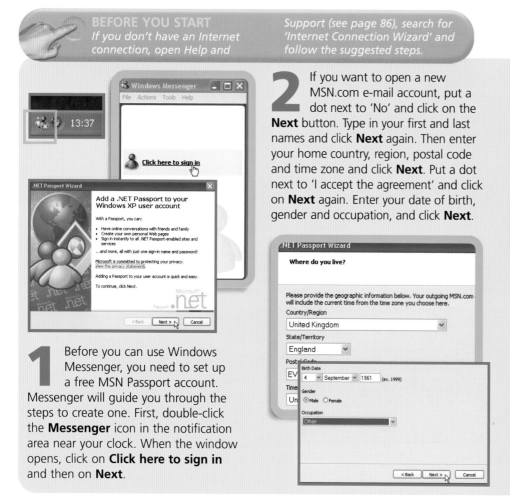

1 Before you can use Windows Messenger, you need to set up a free MSN Passport account. Messenger will guide you through the steps to create one. First, double-click the **Messenger** icon in the notification area near your clock. When the window opens, click on **Click here to sign in** and then on **Next**.

2 If you want to open a new MSN.com e-mail account, put a dot next to 'No' and click on the **Next** button. Type in your first and last names and click **Next** again. Then enter your home country, region, postal code and time zone and click **Next**. Put a dot next to 'I accept the agreement' and click on **Next** again. Enter your date of birth, gender and occupation, and click **Next**.

3 Choose an e-mail address (you will be offered an alternative if the one you want is taken) and click on **Next**. Enter a password, click on **Next** and select a secret question and answer followed by **Next** again. Choose whether you want to share your details or be a part of the Hotmail Member Directory. When the You're done screen appears, click on **Finish**.

Watch out
Never reveal your address, telephone number, bank account or credit card details to anyone in a chat room or individual message window, even if you know the person to whom you are talking.

Do not disturb
If you want to browse the Internet or send and receive e-mail but don't want to be contacted via Messenger, you can set your status as 'Appear Offline'. Then contacts who have you in their contact book will see your name as 'Not Online' and will not be able to initiate chats. Right-click on your name (see right) to set this status.

5 If your contact is online, their name appears in your 'Online' list in the Message window. Right-click on their name and choose **Send an Instant Message** to start an online chat. Type your message in the bottom box and click the **Send** button when you want to transmit it. You can send files too – click on **Send a File or Photo** and choose the file you want to send.

4 Once Messenger has been set up, it will sign you in and you can begin to add your contacts. Click on **Add a contact**, type in their e-mail address and click on **Next**. Click on **Next** at the next screen and on **Finish** at the You're done screen. Now, whenever your contact is online you can chat, exchange files and even share an application window with them.

6 You can use Messenger for video conferencing with relatives abroad and for sharing information at work. Note that some services, such as making phone calls from your PC, require you to sign up and make monthly payments. If you want to chat in real time with more than one person, click on **Go to Chat Rooms** and select a nickname. If you are asked to download an 'Add-in', click on **Yes**.

Keeping Windows up to date

In an ideal world, all software would be perfect and would run without any bugs or crashes. Unfortunately, this isn't always the case. Most programs have minor problems when they are released and Windows is no exception. When Microsoft finds out about a problem, they upload a 'fix', or update, to their Web site, which can be downloaded and installed automatically.

UPDATING WINDOWS
To save you the trouble of regularly checking the Microsoft Web site for new updates, Windows does it for you.

Windows Automatic Updates
By default, when you connect to the Internet, Windows XP automatically checks the Microsoft

Web site and looks for new updates. If any are found, a globe icon appears in your notification area to tell you when an update is available for your PC. Double-click on the icon and a dialogue box asks you if you want to install the updates now. You can select **Remind Me Later** but this box will keep reappearing. It is usually best to install the update by clicking on the **Install** option.

After reading the agreement, click on the **Accept** button and Windows will complete the rest of the process for you. When you are asked which updates you want, only deselect a box if you are certain that you don't need that file. See 'Close up' below for information on how to download updates specific to your PC.

Customising Automatic Updates
To alter how this facility runs, click on the **Start** button, right-click on **My Computer**, choose **Properties** then select the **Automatic Updates** tab in the System Properties box. There are three main options under 'Settings'. Select the first if you want to be notified before downloading any updates. Choose the second

one (the default) if you just want to be notified once they are downloaded. The third option allows you to set a download date and time.

Manually checking for updates
If you choose not to update automatically, you can still download and install the updates manually. Connect to the Internet and click on the **Start** button and **All Programs** followed by **Windows Update**. Then, click on **Scan for updates**. Once the scan has completed you can select the components to download and install.

Installing downloaded items
If you decide against installing an update you have downloaded, Windows will keep the file on your hard drive. Install the file later by selecting the **Automatic Updates** tab in the System Properties box as above, and clicking on the **Declined Updates** button.

Close up
Windows Automatic Updates only downloads critical updates. If you want to check for Windows updates specific to your system, click on the Start **button,** All Programs **and choose** Windows Update. **Follow the instructions on the Web site.**

Good Housekeeping

Maximise your disk space

As you create more and more files and install new programs on your PC, your hard disk will start to fill up. If your hard disk gets too full, you will run out of room to install further programs and your PC may slow down. Keep an eye on how much space you have and regularly delete old folders and files to help keep your PC running smoothly.

SEE ALSO...
- *Deleting files* p 32
- *Uninstall old programs* p 74
- *Maintain your hard disk* p 76

BEFORE YOU START
Look through your documents and decide which ones you need to keep and which ones to delete, if necessary. Make sure anything important is filed in a safe place.

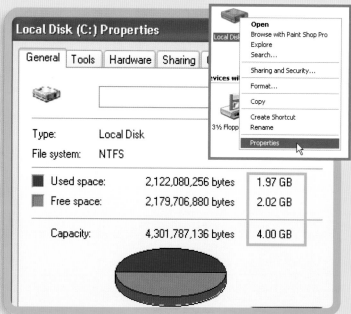

1 To check how much space you have on your hard disk, click on the **Start** button and then select **My Computer**. Click on the **Local Disk** icon in the My Computer window and check under 'Details' to see how much free hard disk space you have.

2 Then right-click on the **Local Disk** icon and choose **Properties**. Under the 'General' tab in the Properties dialogue box, you can see the amount of used and free space, as well as your hard disk capacity. This information is given in numerical and graphical formats. Click **OK** or **Cancel** to close the window.

72

How much space do I need?

For your computer to work efficiently you need to keep a minimum of 200MB of hard disk space free. If you want to install new software, check how much disk space the software requires first. To do this, insert the software CD, set up the installation and look for the screen that tells you how much space you need. If you don't have enough space, either choose to install fewer components (some applications allow you to specify which elements you want to install), or quit the installation by following the on-screen instructions and start from step 3 below.

Space Required on C:	1536 KB
Space Available on C:	2089 MB

Close up
Windows Compressed Folders can reduce the size of certain files without losing any data. This process is known as compression. In any folder, right-click on an empty area, select New *and then* Compressed Folder. *Choose a suitable name and drag files to the folder to create compressed copies, and then delete the originals.*

4 Windows can help you to free up space on your hard disk. Click on the **Start** button, choose **All Programs**, **Accessories**, **System Tools** and then the **Disk Cleanup** tab. Click on the **OK** button and then on **Yes** to start the process. When Disk Cleanup has finished, open the Disk Cleanup window again and click on the **More Options** tab. From here you can remove Windows components or programs you don't use and delete all but the most recent system restore point – see page 100 for information on System Restore.

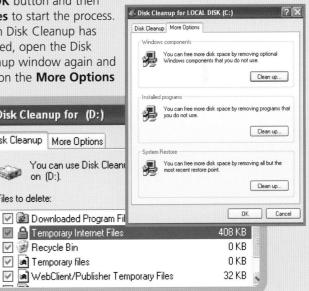

3 If you need to free up some space on your hard disk, you have several options. The first thing to do is to delete unwanted or out-of-date files. Browse your My Documents folder and drag any files you want to delete to the Recycle Bin – see page 32 for more information on deleting files and emptying your Recycle Bin.

Uninstall old programs

Removing programs you no longer use frees up valuable hard disk space, but you need to uninstall them correctly. If you just put them in the Recycle Bin, problems could arise because you may not locate all the relevant files and also Windows would not know the program has been removed. You can safely uninstall most programs using the Add or Remove Programs utility.

SEE ALSO...
- *Create your own shortcuts* p 48
- *Maintain your hard disk* p 76

BEFORE YOU START
Check that the program you intend to remove will not be wanted by other users. Then go to the **Start** menu, **Control Panel**, and **Add or Remove Programs**.

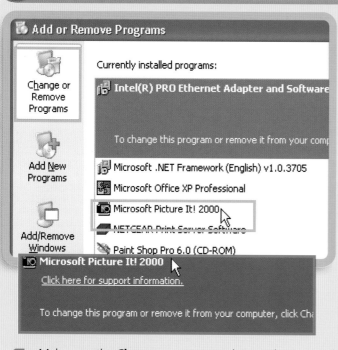

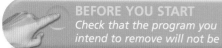

1 Make sure the **Change or Remove Programs** button is selected in the Add or Remove Programs dialogue box. A list of all the programs that can be removed using this process is shown on the right. Scroll down the list and click on the one you want to remove.

2 Click on the **Remove** button. A special uninstallation program, designed for the software you have chosen, will open.

You may be asked to confirm your decision to uninstall. Make sure you've selected the correct program and click on the **Yes** button.

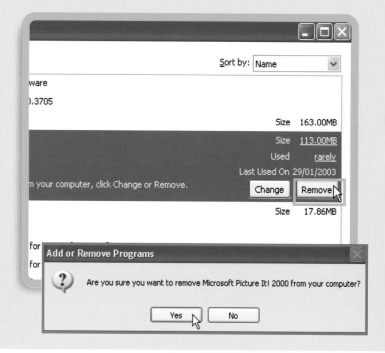

Bright idea
Before you uninstall software, back up any related data you wish to keep. Ensure that you still have the original installation disks in case you want to reinstall the program at a later date.

Deleting other programs
Some programs do not register themselves with Windows and therefore don't show up in the 'Add or Remove Programs' list. If you want to uninstall one of these programs, click on the **Start** button, **All Programs** and then click on the program's folder – it should contain its own uninstallation software. Click on **Uninstall** to start the process.

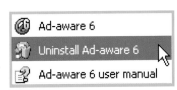

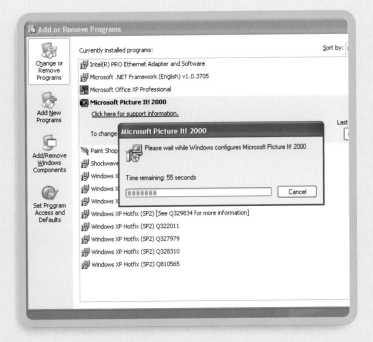

3 Windows will now uninstall all the relevant program files. A dialogue box displays the progress of the operation.

If some program files are shared with other programs, you'll be asked whether you want to remove them. Just to be safe, click on **No**.

4 You may need to remove any unwanted program shortcuts on the Start menu and shortcut icons on your Desktop. Click on the **Start** menu, then **All Programs** and right-click on any shortcut or folder that belongs to an uninstalled program. Select **Delete** and click on **Yes** to confirm deletion of the shortcut. Desktop shortcuts can be dragged to the Recycle Bin.

Maintain your hard disk

To ensure that your hard disk is in optimum health, it's a good idea to perform regular maintenance. Windows has an Error-checking program, which scans your hard disk and other drives for errors, and a Disk Defragmenter, which reorders your data on the hard disk so that files are stored more efficiently. Both these utilities can help keep your PC running smoothly.

SEE ALSO...
● *Program crashes* p 97
● *Reinstalling Windows* p 102

BEFORE YOU START
It can take several hours to run Disk Defragmenter, so make sure you leave plenty of time. You can leave it to run overnight, but ensure all programs are closed.

1 To check a disk for errors, click on the **Start** button and then select **My Computer**. Right-click on the drive you want to check – your hard disk should be C: – and choose **Properties** from the pop-up menu. Click on the **Tools** tab and then click on the **Check Now** button under 'Error-checking'. You can perform a simple disk check by clicking the **Start** button. However, to perform a thorough check, put ticks next to 'Automatically fix file system errors' and 'Scan for and attempt recovery of bad sectors', and then click on the **Start** button.

2 It is not possible for Windows to check a drive that it is currently using, so it schedules the error-checking process to take place next time you start your PC. Click on the **Yes** button to tell Windows to go ahead. Then close all programs and restart your computer. Before Windows has finished loading, a screen is displayed giving you the option to bypass the error check by pressing any key. If you want to go ahead, simply leave your PC and the error-checking will start. This process may take several minutes. The progress will be displayed on screen and your computer will restart automatically when the check is complete.

```
Checking file system on C:
The type of the file system is FAT32.

A disk check has been scheduled.
Windows will now check the disk.
Volume serial number 1234-5678
Windows is verifying files and folders.
9 percent completed......
```

Scheduled tasks

Windows' Scheduled Tasks can prompt you to run Defragmenter. Click on the

Start button, **All Programs**, **Accessories**, **System Tools** and choose **Scheduled Tasks**. Then double-click on **Add Scheduled Task** and click on the **Next** button. At the next screen, click on the **Browse** button and locate the System32 folder within your Windows folder. Then type 'defrag.exe' in the box next to 'File name' and click on **Open**. Put a dot next to 'Monthly' and click **Next**. Choose a date and time, and click **Next** and **Next** again, followed by **Finish**. Close the Scheduled Tasks box.

Key word
Windows often divides files into segments and stores them in various free spaces on the hard disk. This is known as fragmentation. Disk Defragmenter reorders the data.

4 If you need to defragment your disk, make sure that all other programs are closed and you are disconnected from the Internet. Then click on the **Defragment** button to start the Disk Defragmenter. A visual representation of the process is displayed and a barchart at the bottom of the window shows your progress. Click on **Close** when the process has finished. Click on the **View Report** button to see more information on the analysis or about the defragmentation.

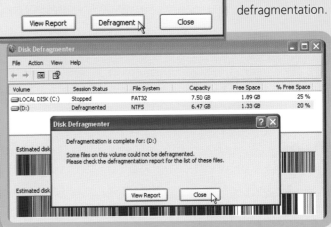

3 You should analyse your hard disk for fragmentation once a month or after installing programs. To defragment your hard disk, you must be logged on as an Administrator (see page 44) and a minimum of 15 per cent free disk space is required. Go to the **Start** menu, and select **All Programs**, **Accessories**, then **System Tools**. Click on **Disk Defragmenter** and then click on **Analyze**. Windows checks your disk, displays a visual representation of the data on your hard disk with a key, and tells you whether you need to defragment it.

Back up your work

To avoid losing important work in the event of a problem with your hard disk, it makes sense to back up your files. When you create a backup, Windows compresses your files and folders and copies them onto a storage disk. You can then update your backup files at regular intervals. This means you can restore your work if files get corrupted.

SEE ALSO...
● *Copy and move files* p 30
● *Create your own shortcuts* p 48
● *Reinstalling Windows* p 102

BEFORE YOU START
Make sure you have adequate storage space for backing up your work. It is best to use either a recordable CD (CD-R) or a Zip disk, if you have a Zip drive.

1 Windows XP Home edition includes the Windows Backup program on its CD-ROM. To install it, put your Windows CD-ROM in the drive, click on the **Start** button and select **My Computer**. Then right-click on your CD-ROM drive icon and choose **Open**. Double-click on **VALUEADD**, followed by **MSFT** and **NTBACKUP**. In the **NTBACKUP** folder, double-click on **NTBACKUP Windows Installer Package** to install Backup.

2 To start Backup, click on the **Start** button, select **All Programs**, **Accessories**, **System Tools** and then **Backup**. When the Backup or Restore Wizard dialogue box appears, click on the **Next** button, put a dot next to 'Back up files and settings' and click on **Next**. In the 'What to back up' panel, choose **My documents and settings**, insert a storage disk in the appropriate drive and click on **Next**.

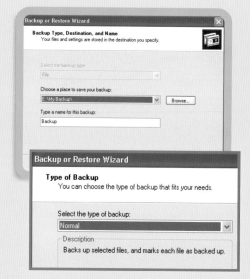

3 Select the drive to which you want to back up your files (click on the **Browse** button if it isn't on the list) and click on **Next**. Then click on the **Advanced** button and make sure **Normal** is selected under 'Select the type of backup'. Click on **Next**, put a tick next to 'Verify data after backup' and click on **Next** again.

Zip and CD-R drives

If you need to back up lots of files on a regular basis, it's worth buying a Zip drive (right) or a CD-R drive, which is a CD-ROM drive that can 'burn' files onto CDs. The disks that come with these drives hold a lot of data. While a floppy disk holds just 1.44MB, a Zip disk comes in 100MB, 250MB and 750MB sizes and a recordable CD holds between 650MB and 700MB of data.

Expert advice

Always carefully label, date and number the disks you use for backing up. To update your backup, run the Backup or Restore Wizard again, but choose **Incremental** under 'Select the type of backup' (see step 3). This time, Backup will add only changed and updated files to your backup file.

5 To restore your data, launch Backup as in step 2 and click on **Next**, but choose 'Restore files and settings' in the Backup or Restore Wizard box and click on **Next**. Then select the files or folders you want to restore by browsing and selecting under 'Items to restore'. Click on the **Next** button and then on **Finish**. Click on **Close** when the restore is complete.

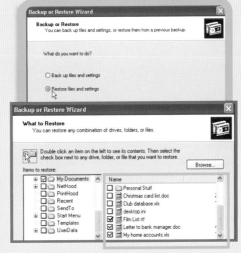

4 Put a dot next to 'Append this backup to the existing backups' and click on **Next**. Then choose whether to run the backup immediately by selecting **Now**, or to schedule it to run at a particular time and date and then at regular intervals afterwards. Make a selection and click on the **Next** button followed by **Finish**. When Backup has completed, click on **Close**.

6 If you prefer, you can be more specific about the files and folders you want to back up. On the first Backup screen, click on the **Advanced Mode** link and select the **Backup** tab. You can now choose a specific folder or files if, for example, you want to back up your accounts files separately from your other data. Select a folder in the left pane and the files in the right pane. Once you've selected the items you want to back up, click on the **Browse** button to choose a location and click on the **Start Backup** button.

Power saving

Although modern PCs are designed to be as energy efficient as possible, they still use a similar amount of electricity to a television. Most PCs come with power saving options and Windows XP has settings that let your PC economise on power if it is left idle for a certain length of time. This not only reduces your electricity bill, but helps save global energy as well.

HOW IT WORKS
You can specify exactly when you would like your computer to go into energy saving mode.

To set Energy Saving on your computer, click on the **Start** button, select **Control Panel** and click on **Performance and Maintenance**. Then select **Power Options**. This opens the Power Options Properties dialogue box.

Power options
There are three levels of power saving: for the monitor, for the hard disk and for the whole system. Select the **Power Schemes** tab and

click the arrow to the right of the 'Power schemes' box. Six options are shown as standard: Home/Office Desk and Portable/Laptop are the two most common options, depending on your PC.

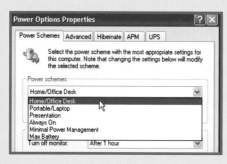

The monitor
Your monitor probably uses more electricity than any other part of your computer but it can be turned off automatically. Click on the arrow

to the right of the 'Turn off monitor' box, scroll down and select a length of time after which the screen will go blank (the green power light on the front of the monitor will change to orange). To restore the screen as it was before this, just move the mouse or press a key on the keyboard. Work and programs are not affected. Experiment to find your own optimum time, but remember not to make it so short that your screen turns off when you are just pausing.

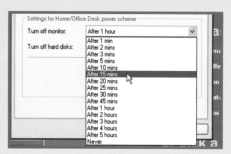

Expert advice
You can name and save different sets of Power Schemes for use at different times, but it is likely that you will decide on one set of timings which suit you best. You can alter your current settings very quickly and easily, or even switch to another set, using the Power Options icon on the Taskbar.

Close up
Most laptops have incorporated power-saving features since their introduction. This is because they need to be portable and it is important that the battery lasts as long as possible when you are on the move.

Hard disks

Now select a similar time for the hard disk. This stops its spinning motion and puts the operating system into a temporary halt mode. It is a good idea to set the hard disk time to a similar time to the standby mode, so they switch off at more or less the same time.

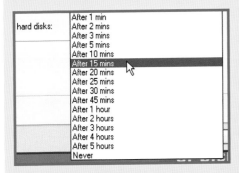

System stand by

This allows your computer system to go into standby mode – a kind of deep sleep. It can be woken up by clicking or moving the mouse, or by pressing a key on the keyboard. Programs and windows are not closed down, so you don't have to restart or wait for Windows to start up. While this is an extremely useful option, do not use it

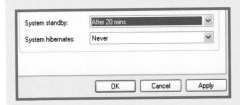

instead of shutting down your computer when you have finished working (unless you are running a maintenance schedule). If you do, and there is a power failure or your computer crashes, then unsaved work in open files will be lost. Click on the arrow beside the 'System stand by' panel, scroll down and select a time. Or you can select 'Never', which will still enable you to set separate power saving for the monitor and the hard disk.

Advanced options

Click on the **Advanced** tab to view` two additional option boxes. The first places a small Power Options icon on the Taskbar – this is useful for quick access to your power saving settings. The second option operates only if you have set up a user password (see page 44). Put a tick here so that, when you leave your machine unattended and it goes into standby, a password will be requested before the PC can be used. This means no-one can access your account without your permission. Once you have chosen your settings, click on the **Apply** button and then on **OK** to confirm them. Before your computer goes into standby mode, a

dialogue box appears warning you that it will do so in 15 seconds. Two buttons offer the choice of cancelling (Cancel Stand by) or proceeding straightaway (Standby Now). If you selected the password option, when you wake up the computer a dialogue box will appear asking you to type in your password.

Save more energy

There are other ways of saving energy and money that you may also wish to consider. For example, you should ensure that there is sufficient space and ventilation around your computer. There is a small fan inside the system unit which cools the hard disk but with less ventilation, this fan needs more energy to run.

Make sure hardware peripherals, such as printers, are switched off unless you are printing a document. If you schedule disk maintenance tasks (see page 76) to run during the night, leave your PC on standby – it will come to life when the task is due to begin.

Changing settings

If you have added the **Power Options** icon to the Taskbar (see above) right-click on it to make changes to your power settings. When the **Adjust Power Properties** button appears, click on it to open the Power Options Properties dialogue box, which you can use to adjust your settings at any time.

Close up
Some PCs have a power feature called 'Hibernate', in which your PC saves open documents to the hard disk before going into a power saving mode. When you restart your PC, your Desktop is restored exactly as you left it. This is useful if you are leaving your PC for an extended period.

Computer viruses

Viruses should always be taken very seriously as they can do a great deal of damage. However, by being careful about the files you allow into your computer and by putting in place certain safeguards, you will greatly reduce the risk of your PC being infected. Powerful virus checking software is available that can check for infected files before you open them.

SEE ALSO...
● *Back up your work p 78*

VIRUSES EXPLAINED
Find out what viruses are, why they exist, how they spread and what you can do to avoid them.

What are viruses?
Viruses are programs or segments of code that run without your knowledge. They are usually disguised and may sit on your computer for some time before activating. This gives them a chance to replicate or spread to programs, files and other connected computers before being discovered. There are all kinds of viruses, with different capabilities and methods of attack.

What can they do to my computer?
Some viruses are relatively harmless – for instance, they may cause a message to appear on your screen for no apparent reason. But other viruses aim to damage files so that you may lose some of your work or, worse still, they may damage vital Windows files, so you have to reinstall your system.

Who creates viruses and why?
Viruses are deliberately programmed by people who set out to spread them to as many computers as possible. There are many reasons why they do this. They could have political and ideological motives: a virus can be a protest against a government or market dominance. Or it might be an ego trip for someone who wishes to prove themselves cleverer than the software engineers.

How could I catch a virus?
Like a cold, a computer virus has to be caught, so it has to get into your PC from an external source. Such sources include:
External drives: If you often use floppy disks, CD-ROMs or other removable disks, you could unwittingly open an infected file. A friend could give you a virus without even realising it.
The Web: You should download files from reputable sites only. Legitimate Web sites should state that they use anti-virus software to check all downloadable files and programs.
E-mail: The most common way to catch a virus is via an e-mail attachment. An attachment is a self-contained data file sent with an e-mail. When an e-mail includes an attachment, a paperclip is displayed beside the e-mail details (see below). Typically, you need to click on the paperclip to open and view the attachment. Only open an attachment if you know the person who sent it and are sure that they intended to send you the file.

To: kevin@plan.co.uk

Close up
Not all CD-ROMS are a potential risk. Those from reputable software companies are unlikely to contain viruses. However, you should be cautious when using recordable or rewritable CDs created on another person's PC.

Watch out
E-mail is a popular vehicle for viruses. But downloading an e-mail will not allow a virus to spread; you have to open the message or attachment. Unfortunately, most e-mail software automatically displays the contents of a message so, if you use e-mail, it is important to protect your system with anti-virus software.

TYPES OF VIRUS

Viruses take various forms and can attack your computer's files in different ways. Here are some of the main culprits.

File infector

This is a virus that attaches itself to program files. Program files are 'executable', which means that if you open the file, you launch a program. So if you don't open the file, the virus cannot run. Be suspicious of e-mail attachments or unverifiable downloads ending in '.exe', '.com', '.vbx' or '.bat', but also be aware that files created by programs such as Word and Excel could easily carry a macro virus. Windows will warn you about viruses when you start a download.

Boot sector virus

The boot sector contains files that tell your computer how to load the operating system each time you start up. If you insert a floppy disk containing a boot sector virus into your computer, you will be able to read files on the disk without a problem. However, if you restart your PC with the floppy disk still in the drive, your PC will access it, run the virus, and then may stop working. You should always avoid leaving a floppy disk in the drive when you turn off your computer. Check your BIOS manual for information on boot sector virus protection.

Multipartite virus

Like file infectors, these viruses attach themselves to program files. When activated, they attack your hard drive's boot sector, so that the computer doesn't know how to find and load the operating system. This makes it impossible to start up your computer. Luckily, these viruses are hard to program and rare.

Macro virus

Some programs, such as Word and Excel, enable you to create macros, which are a series of instructions that you set up. Anyone with knowledge of the Visual Basic programming language can create a macro virus. If you open a Word or Excel file containing a macro virus, it will spread to other Word or Excel files on your PC.

Macro viruses are common but easy to avoid. When you open a file containing a macro, both Word and Excel display a box telling you macros are present. Unless you're sure where they came from, click the **Disable Macros** button.

Worm

A virus can replicate itself, but to move from computer to computer, the user has to pass on the infected file. Worms, on the other hand, can spread themselves.

The famous worm trick is to e-mail itself to everyone in your Address Book. Computer networks are particularly vulnerable, as viruses can spread in a very short space of time.

Trojan horse

These pretend to be harmless, even useful, applications. Then, when you least expect it, something nasty happens. Trojan horses are not classified as viruses because they cannot replicate themselves to infect other files on your computer.

Virus hoaxes

If you use e-mail, you are probably used to virus warnings. Unfortunately, it's hard to know when these are genuine and when they are just practical jokes. The danger of hoaxes is that you may start to ignore real warnings. Combat this by looking up the latest viruses on reputable Web sites, such as www.mcafee.com and www.symantec.com.

I Love You

In the year 2000, the infamous worm 'I Love You' brought computers and networks to a halt all over the world. It arrived as an e-mail file attachment called 'LOVE-LETTER-FOR-YOU.TEXT.vbs'. When the recipient opened the file, it read through the Address Book on that person's computer and forwarded itself to all the e-mail addresses it had read. Although it only affected Microsoft Outlook and Outlook Express, the 'I Love You' worm managed to spread around the world in a matter of hours, damaging data on millions of PCs and blocking up company networks with unwanted e-mails. The culprit was a young programmer in the Far East.

AVOIDING VIRUSES

There are many ways to safeguard your computer from being infected with a disruptive virus.

Anti-virus programs

These programs protect you against thousands of known viruses. The two best known applications are McAfee Virus Scan and Norton AntiVirus from Symantec.

You can set up your anti-virus program to run in the background, so that it keeps regular checks on your computer and vets all incoming e-mails and external disks, such as floppies and CDs.

Alternatively, you can run a virus check manually and choose exactly which drive and which files you want it to scan. Generally, the first place to look is the C: drive, where your operating system files are saved.

You've found a virus

When you run a scan, a log file documents the results. You can check this file at any time.

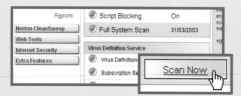

If your anti-virus program finds an infected file, you need to decide what to do with it. The file can be moved to a separate folder, deleted, or noted and left. Your program may be able to clean the file, so that you can carry on using it. However, the safest option is to quarantine it.

Free updates

New viruses appear all the time, which is why the Web support provided by your software manufacturer is vital. Anti-virus programmers spend their working lives looking for viruses and creating fixes. Often you never hear about a virus because a fix is made before it spreads. Both McAfee and Symantec provide the latest anti-virus lists and software as automatic updates, similar to Windows Update. You can also sign up for e-mail newsletters, keeping you up to date on any new viruses for which fixes have not yet been created.

Better safe than sorry

Anti-virus software wards off most viruses, but there are additional steps you can take to keep your PC clean:

1 Keeping all of your software up to date helps beat hackers. Microsoft sometimes issues patches for program loopholes on its Web site

(see page 70). And you should check your other software manufacturers' Web sites regularly for updates and patches.

2 Back up your hard drive regularly (see page 78) and make sure you have the original disks for your programs and operating system. If a virus infects your computer and you lose everything, you'll need to reinstall the software and all your data.

3 If you don't have the latest version of your anti-virus software, try an online virus scanning service, such as HouseCall from Trend Micro (www.housecall.antivirus.com/pc_housecall).

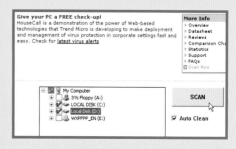

4 Beware of e-mail attachments, even if they are from a friend. Avoid downloadable newsgroup files, and only download files from reputable Web sites.

5 Set up safety settings on your Web browser. For instance, you can choose to be prompted should you start to download a file by mistake. If you are using Internet Explorer, click on the **Tools** menu and select **Internet Options** and then the **Security** tab. Click the **Custom Level** or **Default Level** buttons to adjust your settings.

Internet Connection Firewall

Windows XP comes with Internet Connection Firewall (ICF), which provides protection against attacks on your PC while you are browsing the Internet. ICF is activated by default when a new Internet dial-up connection is set up. To check that ICF is running, click on the **Start** button, **Network Places** and select **Properties**. Then right-click on the Internet connection, select **Properties** and then the **Advanced** tab. Make sure there's a tick next to 'Protect my computer and network by limiting or preventing access to this computer from the Internet' and click on **OK**.

Troubleshooting

Getting help

If you encounter a problem with Windows or if you want to learn more about your hardware or software settings, consult Windows XP's Help and Support facility. It contains definitions, step-by-step troubleshooters and Internet links for the latest information. If you need further assistance, there are plenty of other avenues to explore as well.

SEE ALSO...
- *Windows won't start up* p 90
- *Error messages* p 94

HELP AND SUPPORT

In most cases, you won't need to look any further than Windows' own Help and Support files to find the solution to your computer queries and problems.

Finding your way around

To access the Windows Help and Support resources, click on the **Start** button and select **Help and Support**. Topics are arranged under headings, on which you can click in the same way as you do with links on a Web site.

Clicking on a heading reveals a comprehensive list of related options – and you can view a pop-up description of each link by hovering

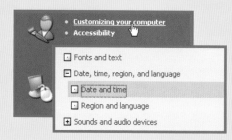

your mouse pointer over it. Once you click on a heading to explore a subject, a panel opens on the left side of the window. You can access sections by clicking on the options, and sub-sections by clicking on the plus signs next to the topics (when clicked they turn into minus signs; click again to close the sub-section).

Continue selecting options until you locate the exact topic for which you are looking. Then select the sub-topic from the pane on the right of the window.

If you get lost, the Home button always returns you to the first window that appears when you open Help and Support. The Back, Forward, Favorites and History buttons help you navigate around the Help windows.

Expert advice

If a program designed to run under an older version of Windows doesn't work, you can run the Program Compatibility Wizard to make it run under Windows XP. Open Help and Support, search for 'compatible' and click on **Getting older programs to run on Windows XP**. Then click on **Start the Program Compatibility Wizard**.

Index button

The index bypasses the topic headings and allows you to access the Help database directly to search for a word. As you start typing in the box under 'Type in the keyword to find', the list is filtered according to the letters you enter. When you locate the topic for which

you are searching, either double-click on it or select it and click on the **Display** button to see the information in the right-hand pane.

Options button

This button opens a pane containing two ways to configure Windows Help – you can change the way the toolbars and links look and also customise the scope of the search facility.

Pick a Help topic

All the subjects covered in Help and Support are grouped on the left under 'Pick a Help topic'. These include using the Internet, printing and

faxing, and troubleshooting problems. As you click on each heading, a new window opens displaying a further list of options.

Ask for assistance

As long as you are connected to the Internet, Windows XP allows other Windows XP users anywhere in the world, to whom you have granted access, to connect to your PC and see exactly what you see on your screen. This is called 'Remote Assistance'. Friends who are more experienced in using Windows, or who know about the particular issue on which you need help, can talk you through solving the problem or even control your mouse pointer from their computer.

You can also connect to Windows XP newsgroups. These are huge searchable databases of users' questions and experts' answers. First search for your topic and read any relevant answers. If you can't find the information you need, post a question and then check back after a day or two for replies.

Pick a task

Under this heading you can find four topics to help you keep your PC running smoothly.

You can initiate a scan for updates to Windows (see page 70) or look for compatible hardware, for instance if you are thinking of buying a new soundcard or graphics adaptor. You can also access System Restore (see page 100) from this section and select from a list of useful tools to help you resolve all sorts of Windows problems.

Did you know?

This section is updated if you are connected to the Internet when you launch Help and Support. Its contents vary according to material supplied from Microsoft. It's worth checking these links for useful information and Windows hints and tips.

Search

The feature that you will probably use most is Search in the top left-hand corner of the Help and Support window. Type in a keyword for the problem you are experiencing and click on the green arrow or press **Return**. If there is a related Help topic, it will be listed in the left-hand panel.

If there are a lot of results, you can refine your search by telling Windows what not to search for. For instance, if you want information on printing but not general advice about printers, you can enter 'printing not printers'.

Close up
If you type two words in the Search box, the search returns a list of Help references which include both words. If you want to extend your search to include all references to each word, type the word 'or' between them.

Troubleshooters

When a feature does not work, Windows offers a specific type of help called a 'troubleshooter'. This asks you a series of in-depth questions that guide you step by step through the possible causes of the problem and help you to repair it. You can also go directly to the Troubleshooting section of Help and Support by typing 'troubleshooter' in the Search box, clicking on the green arrow, selecting **Full-text Search Matches** and clicking on **List of troubleshooters**. A complete list of Windows' troubleshooters will be displayed on the right. Subjects covered by troubleshooters include audio-visual problems, Internet and modem problems, hardware issues and general Windows queries.

The Modem Troubleshooter

A common problem that is encountered when trying to connect to the Internet is your modem not being able to communicate with your ISP (Internet Service Provider). If this occurs, try the

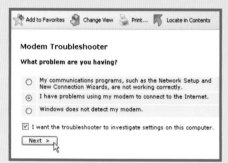

Modem Troubleshooter. It asks you to check whether your modem has been installed correctly, whether you are getting a dial tone, what the various settings are, and so on. Then it talks you step by step through fixing the problem. If it doesn't solve the problem, the troubleshooter advises you to contact the manufacturer, who will invariably ask you the same questions, so it's worth making a note of the answers while using the troubleshooter.

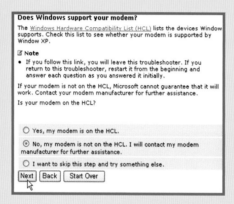

Following instructions

When using a Windows troubleshooter, it is important to answer all the questions and to carry out all the instructions on each page before clicking on the **Next** button to proceed. Otherwise you may carry out an inappropriate repair. If you make a mistake, click on **Back** to return to the previous question or, if you get stuck, click on the **Start Over** button to return to the beginning of the troubleshooter.

OTHER SOURCES OF HELP

Don't give up if Windows Help and Support hasn't provided you with the information you require. You can easily find more help in a host of other locations.

What's This?

Some windows and dialogue boxes offer a handy localised help tool, identified by a question mark box in the top right-hand corner next to the 'Close' button.

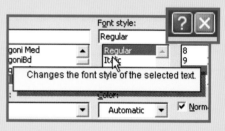

Click on the question mark, then on the item you want to know more about. A small box pops up with information about the item. To close it click again.

Help with programs

Every program has a Help menu of its own. These usually operate in a similar way to Windows Help and Support, letting you locate a topic through clickable links, an index or by typing in a keyword. Microsoft Office programs also offer help via the Office Assistant, a friendly search tool.

Close up
You can also get help on a problem by connecting to the Internet and typing a brief description of the problem in your Internet search engine. Try www.google.co.uk for useful links to help and assistance.

You can launch a Help file without running its program by opening it in Windows Explorer. Go to the **Start** menu, select **All Programs**, **Accessories** and **Windows Explorer**. Locate the file inside the program folder – its icon is usually a blue circle with a question mark, and it may have '.chm' or '.hlp' after the name – and double-click on it to display its contents.

dialer   fonts   display

charmap   defrag   freecell

Readme files

When you buy a program or get one free on a CD attached to the cover of a computer magazine, you will usually find a text file called 'README' accompanies it. Locate this file using Windows' Search facility (see page 34) or by browsing through the program's folder using Windows Explorer. Readme files usually explain

Paint Shop Pro 6.0
Release Notes

Thank you for purchasing Jasc Paint Shop Pro™ 6! Our newest release of Paint Shop Pro is packed with powerful new features and enhancements, including Jasc Animation Shop™ 2. Once you begin using these programs, we think you will see just how easy it can be to create Web graphics and enhance digital photos.

Please remember that this is a licensed version of Paint Shop Pro, and cannot be freely distributed. See the license agreement information included in this document for limits on copying this software and other important information.

CONTENTS
Changes in Paint Shop Pro 6.0
Changes in Animation Shop 2.0
Obtaining and Installing Direct Digital Camera Support
Using the Picture Tube Converter
Paint Shop Pro User Frequently Asked Questions

new features not covered in the manual or Help file, or instructions on how to install the software properly. However, some Readme files include troubleshooting tips for problems discovered as a result of testing and running the program. To view a Readme file, double-click on it and it will open in Notepad, WordPad or Internet Explorer, depending on the type of file.

Calling for help

If all else fails, you may have to resort to asking for help. If you bought your computer equipment from a specialist shop, contact them first when things go wrong, particularly if it is still under guarantee. They might have come across your problem before and be able to offer a solution.

Alternatively, ask the computer manufacturer. Most have Web sites with detailed **FAQs** (Frequently Asked Questions), which might resolve the problem.

If you are having trouble connecting to the Internet, check that your service provider is not experiencing difficulties, then contact your modem manufacturer.

Contacting Microsoft

If you have recently upgraded to Windows XP and are experiencing difficulties not covered by Help and Support, go to Microsoft's Support Web site at http://www.support.microsoft.com.

| Request Support - Overview |
| Submit Incidents Online |
| Telephone Numbers |
| How to Purchase Microsoft Contracts |

You'll find a large number of FAQs, which might provide the right information. If not, you can click on the International Support link. Select your country from the drop-down list and click on the green arrow, then click on **Request Support** on the left and select **Telephone Numbers**. Finally click on **Telephone Microsoft** to view the number of your local Technical Support line. Note that some services require payment, and you will need to give them your 20-digit product code.

System information

Technicians may ask for details of your PC's system. To find this information, click on the **Start** button then **All Programs**, **Accessories**, **System Tools** and **System Information**. On the left is a list of headings. Click on a heading to display information about it in the right pane.

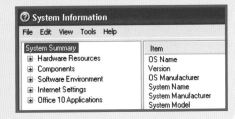

Key word

Almost every software Web site has a page of FAQs *– Frequently Asked Questions – and their answers. Reading through FAQs can be a quick way to find solutions to problems. At the same time, you might also discover lots of other hints that will enhance the use of your computer.*

Windows won't start up

Although Windows XP is an extremely stable and reliable operating system, there are still times when it can let you down. Fortunately, Windows has a wide range of repair programs and online help facilities, including interactive troubleshooter wizards. And if Windows won't run at all, you can start it in a special diagnostic mode called 'Safe Mode'.

SEE ALSO...
- *Getting help* p 86
- *System Restore* p 100
- *Reinstalling Windows* p 102

SAFE MODE

If you are experiencing problems with starting up Windows, Safe Mode is a special Windows state that will enable you to access and use all the Windows troubleshooting facilities.

If Windows won't start up normally, the chances are that the next time you turn your PC on, Windows will run automatically in Safe Mode. This is a simplified level of operation that gives you a limited version of Windows to work with. It temporarily disables all but the most important drivers and devices, as these could be the cause of the problem.

If your PC does not automatically go into Safe Mode, you can force it to do so by intervening during the startup process. Switch on the computer and press and hold down the **F8** key on your keyboard immediately, before

the Windows XP introductory screen appears. Keep pressing the key until you see the text-only Windows Startup menu – this offers you a list of startup options. Select **Safe Mode** by moving to it using the up and down arrow keys, then press the **Enter** key. Your PC will start to load Windows XP in Safe Mode.

The Safe Mode screen

When Windows has loaded, a warning message appears. Click on **Yes** to load the Windows Safe

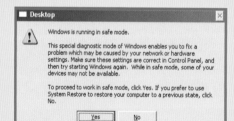

Mode Desktop. The icons and the Taskbar may appear larger than normal and the Desktop background will be black.

Only use Safe Mode for diagnosing startup problems (see opposite). Once you have resolved the problem, restart your computer and Windows should start in normal mode automatically.

Close up
If you start your PC in Safe Mode you will not be able to access your printer and other external devices because the files needed to communicate with these devices will not be loaded.

SOURCES FOR HELP

You don't need to be an expert to use these problem-solving methods. With the help provided by Windows you can work through most problems yourself.

Windows XP Troubleshooter

This facility is part of the Help and Support system, which uses a Windows wizard (a step-by-step guide) to analyse the problem you're having and to come up with a solution.

To access the wizard, click on the **Start** menu and then click **Help and Support**. The Help and Support window appears. Next, type 'troubleshooter' in the Search box to the left of the window, and click on the green arrow.

In the search results list, click on **Full-text Search Matches** and then on **List of troubleshooters**. In the pane on the right, click on the **Startup/Shutdown** link. Then put a dot next to 'My computer stops responding when I try to start Windows' and click on **Next**.

The first suggestion as to what the problem is appears in the right pane with a course of action to remedy it. If this doesn't work, you'll be taken through other options, one at a time, until you find a solution.

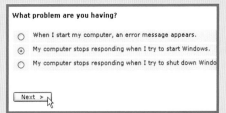

Troubleshooting online

If Windows' troubleshooting wizards can't solve your problem, you can find further information and help at Microsoft's Web site: http://support.microsoft.com.

Expert advice

If you always make sure that you shut down your computer correctly and that you properly uninstall applications you no longer use, you should be able to limit problems with the Windows operating system. Regular hard disk maintenance, such as Error-checking and Disk Defragmenter (see page 76) also help.

Windows won't close down

Occasionally, you may find that your mouse pointer won't move, or that your keyboard doesn't seem to work. This is a problem known as 'freezing'. Fixing a frozen program is fairly simple because you can still access your Help and Support files. But if Windows freezes, you won't be able to use any of the menus or carry out normal program functions.

SEE ALSO...
- *Getting help* p 86
- *System Restore* p 100
- *Reinstalling Windows* p 102

EMERGENCY SHUTDOWN
Often, when Windows freezes, normal commands can't be carried out. In this case you need to follow a special procedure to shut down.

If your computer freezes, press the **Ctrl + Alt + Delete** keys simultaneously. If the keyboard is still working, this opens the Windows Task Manager dialogue box, which lists all of the programs currently running.

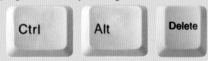

You have two choices – you can either click on the **Shut Down** menu and choose **Turn Off** to switch off or **Restart** to restart your PC, or click on the **Applications** tab and close any individual programs that you're running. To do

this, select each one in the main panel and click on the **End Task** button.

Close running programs
A dialogue box may appear asking if you want to save changes to your open documents. Click on **Yes**. If you have Internet Explorer open, you should close this last as it won't contain any open documents that you need to save. If the

End Program dialogue box appears, click on the **End Now** button.

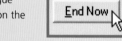

Sometimes, closing programs in this way can resolve the problem, as it may just be due to a software conflict between two of the programs you are running. Thus, when one is closed the other starts to function normally. If this doesn't work, try restarting your computer.

If the problem persists even after restarting, go to Help and Support and run one of the Windows troubleshooters to diagnose and solve your problem. Click on the **Start** button and then on **Help and Support**.

Reset your PC
If Windows won't shut down when you press the **Ctrl + Alt + Delete** keys, press the **Reset** button on your system unit. If your PC has no Reset button, press and hold the **Power** button for a few seconds to switch the computer off and wait for about a minute before you switch it on again.

USING THE TROUBLESHOOTER

Windows offers its own step-by-step assistance to help you establish why problems are occurring.

The Help and Support feature is a good place to start finding out why Windows might have trouble closing down, and to get a solution. When the Help and Support Center window appears, open the list of troubleshooters by searching for 'troubleshooter' and following the instructions detailed on page 88 of this book. Click on the **Startup/Shutdown** link. In the right-hand pane, put a dot next to 'My computer stops responding when I try to shut down Windows' and then click on the **Next** button.

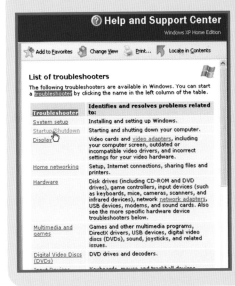

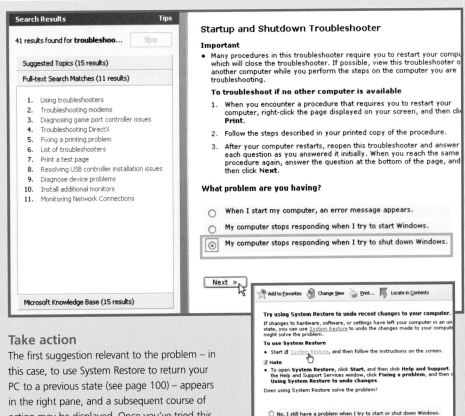

Take action

The first suggestion relevant to the problem – in this case, to use System Restore to return your PC to a previous state (see page 100) – appears in the right pane, and a subsequent course of action may be displayed. Once you've tried this, you are asked if it solved the problem. If not, put a dot next to the appropriate answer and then click on the **Next** button. Further suggestions will be given. Although time-consuming, the troubleshooter offers solutions in a succinct and clear manner that can help you address a host of hardware and software problems.

Close up
Where possible, restart or shut down your computer by clicking on the Start *button,* Turn Off Computer *and then* Restart *or* Turn Off*. This means that all Windows' settings are saved and each program closes properly before Windows shuts down.*

Bright idea
If you cannot solve a problem using the Windows troubleshooters, try using System Restore (see page 100). Or, as a last resort, you may have to reinstall Windows. See page 102 for details.

Error messages

Windows will usually warn you of a system or application problem by displaying an error message on your screen. These messages are there to help you and should never be ignored. Often, they not only describe the error, but suggest a reason for it and how to resolve it. Here are some of the most common error messages, and what you can do about them.

SEE ALSO...
- *Uninstall old programs* p 74
- *Maintain your hard disk* p 76
- *Back up your work* p 78

SOFTWARE HICCUPS
There are many types of software error message. Fortunately, most of these problems are easy to fix.

'File in Use'
If you try to open a file that is already open in a different program, you may get a message saying that it is either locked for editing by another user, being used by another user, or that it is in use by another application and cannot be opened. Just save and close the open version.

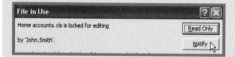

'Error Deleting File or Folder'
This message may appear if you have tried to delete a file that is still open. Check through the

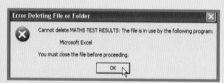

files on your Desktop and Taskbar, close the one you wish to delete and drag it to the Recycle Bin. If the message occurs when deleting files on removable media, such as a Zip, floppy disk or memory card, the disk or memory card may be write-protected. Take it out, push down the tab, put it back in the drive and try again.

'File Corruption'
If one of your files has become corrupted, the only option is to delete it. If it is a program file, the program may cease to function or may behave inconsistently. In this case, reinstall the program from the program CDs to prevent further problems.

'Sharing Violation'
An error message that says 'Sharing Violation' or 'You don't have permission to open this file' has two possible causes. You may be trying to open the file in two programs at the same time (see 'File in Use') or the file may be corrupted (see 'File Corruption').

'Access is denied'
If you get a message telling you that a file cannot be copied over or deleted because access is denied, this means that it may be one of your computer's vital system files. These are guarded by a utility called 'Windows File Protection' to prevent you from making unauthorised changes or deleting the wrong files.

> Cannot delete authz: Access is denied.
>
> Make sure the disk is not full or write-protected and that the file is not currently in use.

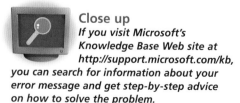

Close up
If you visit Microsoft's Knowledge Base Web site at http://support.microsoft.com/kb, *you can search for information about your error message and get step-by-step advice on how to solve the problem.*

Bright idea
Performing disk maintenance tasks on a regular basis helps to reduce the risk of your *files being corrupted and keeps your PC running smoothly (see page 76).*

How to avoid error messages
- Always use the Add or Remove Programs utility on the Control Panel to uninstall programs.
- Don't move or rename program files and folders.
- Don't move or rename files in your Windows System folder or its sub-folders.
- When you move or rename a file that has a shortcut, delete the old shortcut and create a new one.
- Exit programs when you've finished using them.

MAKING SENSE OF MESSAGES
Some errors can be a little more problematic. Find out what they are and how to steer clear of them.

Missing or out-of-date files
Messages regarding files that are missing or out of date can appear if a file has been accidentally deleted, renamed or overwritten. This can occur if you move a file after creating a shortcut,

rename a program folder or a file in a program folder, or rename an item in your System folder. It also happens when you delete a program file using the Recycle Bin instead of the Add or Remove Programs utility.

However, the main reason you might encounter error messages is that when you install new software or upgrade old software, it can cause conflicts with programs already installed on your computer.

Installing new software
If you install a new program or upgrade, you may get error messages when launching other software. This may be caused by incorrect program or system files or by an incorrect Registry entry. To fix these problems, you can reinstall or repair the software that has ceased to function correctly – Microsoft Office has a repair feature, which scans for files that have been

updated and replaces them with the originals. Just put the Office CD in the drive and follow the onscreen instructions.

You can also run System Restore (see page 100) to return to a previous working state. After running System Restore you will need to reinstall any software and hardware added after the selected restore point. If this doesn't work, try reinstalling Windows (see page 102). This does not affect your previously installed program files or data. Consult the manufacturer's Web site for the latest fixes and patches, and for information on how to avoid problems during and after installation. Try to buy hardware and software that has been designed for Windows XP. This information should be visible on the manufacturer's packaging, or you can find a hardware and software compatibility list on Microsoft's Web site at www.microsoft.com.

Watch out
Occasionally you may experience a crash followed by a blue screen with white text. If this happens after you've installed new software, there may be a conflict with Windows. Restart your PC and try again. Use System Restore (see page 100) if the error persists. If you don't understand the message, write it down and contact your local PC specialist for advice.

Key word
A driver is a program that translates data between the Windows operating system and a piece of hardware, such as your printer. It enables the hardware item to work in conjunction with your PC.

Bright idea
If you don't know what caused your error message, make a note of what it says and when it occurred so you can perform a search for it on the Internet or report the problem accurately to the manufacturer.

YOUR HARD DISK

Not all problems are caused by your software. Here are some common hard disk and hardware issues.

Error-checking messages

Windows' built-in maintenance tools include an Error-checking utility (see page 76). It checks your hard disk for problems and attempts to fix them. When it finds an error it displays a message and, in most cases, fixes it before it can cause serious problems. If the Error-checking tool has detected errors that it cannot

fix, contact your PC dealer. If it doesn't find any problems, you will see a message that reads 'Windows has checked the file system and found no problems'.

Hardware issues

Many error messages arise from a hardware conflict. This is when two devices, such as your modem and printer, try to access the same

> **Fix a Problem**
> - Diagnosing game port controller issues
> - Hardware Troubleshooter
> - Getting o[ld] programs to [r]un on Windows XP

resources simultaneously. To solve this type of problem, use the Windows troubleshooters (see page 88). Go to the **Start** menu and select **Help and Support**. Type 'hardware troubleshooter' in the 'Search' box and click the green arrow. Click on the **Hardware**

Troubleshooter link that appears on the left of the window. The troubleshooter will appear on the right, offering step-by-step guidance.

If you still get error messages, the problem may be the **driver** for your hardware device. Contact the device manufacturer for the latest driver. You may be able to download it for free from the manufacturer's Web site.

Running out of disk space

Occasionally you may see a message saying your hard disk is getting full. Simply run Disk Cleanup to delete redundant and temporary files (see page 73).

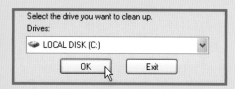

Program crashes

When a program crashes, your mouse pointer turns into an hourglass icon and you won't be able to type or access any of the menus. If this is the case, you will need to exit the program and you may lose any work that you haven't saved. Some crashes may just be momentary glitches, but if they reoccur regularly, you should reinstall the program.

SEE ALSO...
- *Maintain your hard disk* p 76
- *Back up your work* p 78
- *Getting help* p 86

BEFORE YOU START
Try clicking on the red Close Program button at the top right of your program window. If this doesn't work, press **Alt + F4**. If this also fails, follow the steps below.

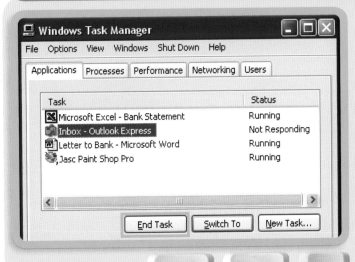

2 If the program closes, exit the Task Manager, launch the program again and resume working. If Task Manager can't close the program, another dialogue box will open. Click on **End Now**. If you have to do this, you should restart Windows. Occasionally, more than one program may have crashed, so you may need to revisit the applications list in the Windows Task Manager dialogue box. If you didn't save work on the document you were using before the crash, you will lose it when you exit the program.

If exiting the program hasn't worked and you still can't do anything on your computer, consult the instructions on page 92.

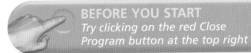

1 You'll know when a program has crashed because you won't be able to use its menus. However, if you move the mouse away from the program window, you may find it reverts from an hourglass to a pointer. Press the **Ctrl + Alt + Delete** keys. This brings up the Windows Task Manager box, which lists all the programs running on your PC. Select the program that is not responding and click on the **End Task** button.

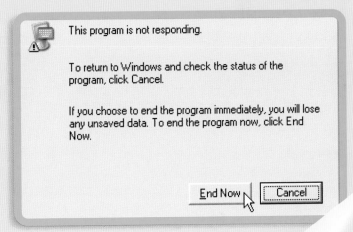

This program is not responding.

To return to Windows and check the status of the program, click Cancel.

If you choose to end the program immediately, you will lose any unsaved data. To end the program now, click End Now.

End Now   Cancel

Key word

Temporary files **store** *information about a program currently in use and should be deleted automatically when you close the program that created them. However, if you crash they are retained on your hard disk.*

Close up

To reduce the risk of losing data in a crash, some programs allow you to save data automatically at set intervals. In Word, click on the Tools *menu and then* Options. *Then click on the* Save *tab and select a time in the 'Save AutoRecover info every' box. Click on* OK.

CLEARING OUT TEMPORARY FILES

1 If your PC frequently crashes, your hard disk may become cluttered with **temporary files**. You can clear these out by performing a search for them and deleting them. Click on the **Start** button, select **Search**, and then **All Files and folders**. In the panel under 'All or part of the file name', type '*.tmp'. In the 'Look in' panel make sure 'Local Hard Drives (C:)' is selected and click on **Search**.

2 The right-hand pane displays all files ending in '.tmp'. To delete multiple files, hold down the **Ctrl** key and click on the files one at a time – avoid selecting files in the Windows folders. Then right-click on the files, choose **Delete** and click on **Yes**. Note that you may only be able to delete one file at a time as some may be in use.

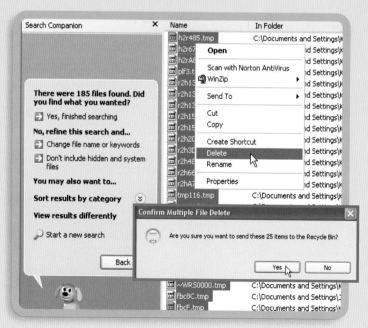

Reinstalling a problem program

If a program persistently crashes, you should uninstall it. Click on the **Start** menu and select **Control Panel**. Click on the **Add or Remove Programs** link, then on the program, and follow the onscreen instructions. Then restart your PC and install the program from scratch. Place the program's CD-ROM in the drive. If the install program doesn't run automatically, click on the **Start** button, select **My Computer**, and then click on the **CD-ROM** icon followed by the **Setup** icon.

4 In the next dialogue box, the 'Disk Cleanup' tab will be selected by default. In the panel below, put a tick next to 'Temporary files'. Look at the rest of the options to see if there is anything else you would like to clear from your hard drive, then click on the **OK** button. In the next box click on **Yes**. Disk Cleanup will then delete the '.tmp' files. A panel shows the progress.

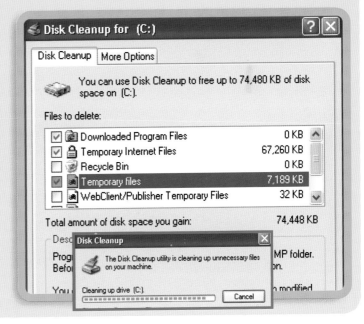

3 You can get Windows to automatically remove temporary files over seven days old using Disk Cleanup. Click on the **Start** menu and select **All Programs**, then **Accessories**.

Select **System Tools** and click on **Disk Cleanup**. A dialogue box appears, with your hard disk (normally C:) selected. Click on the **OK** button. A panel shows the progress of the cleanup operation.

System Restore

Sometimes a computer may develop a problem, such as freezing, immediately after you have installed new software or hardware. If the problem proves difficult to resolve, you can retrieve your previous working setup by using the Windows XP System Restore feature. This tool winds back the clock to an earlier time when your PC was running smoothly.

SEE ALSO...
● *Uninstall old programs* p 74

BEFORE YOU START
System Restore will help you return your PC to good health.

Click on the **Start** menu and select **All Programs, Accessories, System Tools** and then **System Restore**.

1 When the System Restore Wizard opens and the welcome screen appears, put a dot next to 'Restore my computer to an earlier time' in the panel on the right, then click on the **Next** button.

2 Select the most recent date when you know your PC was working properly. To scroll through the calendar, click the arrow buttons in the top corners. You can only select dates that are highlighted in dark blue – these are the days your computer saved a Restore Point. Then look in the panel on the right and choose one of the restore points for that date, and click on **Next**.

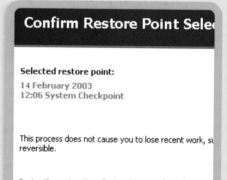

1. On this calendar, click a bold date.

<	February 2003					>
Mon	Tue	Wed	Thu	Fri	Sat	Sun
27	28	29	30	31	1	2
3	4	5	6	7	8	9
10	11	12	13	**14**	**15**	**16**
17	18	19	20	21	22	23
24	25	26	27	28	1	2
3	4	5	6	7	8	9

2. On this list, click a restore point.

<	14 February 2003
12:06:35 System Checkpoint	

Confirm Restore Point Sele

Selected restore point:
14 February 2003
12:06 System Checkpoint

This process does not cause you to lose recent work, su reversible.

During the restoration, System Restore shuts down Wir restarts using the settings from the date and time listed

3 If the wizard prompts you to do so, close any running programs then click on **OK**. Click on **Next** to restore your Windows to the state it was at on the date and time you selected. Once restoration is complete, your PC will restart and a 'Restoration Complete' message will be displayed. You must now reinstall any programs and Windows Updates that had been installed since the restore point.

SYSTEM RESTORE

By undoing certain changes you have made to your computer after a chosen date, System Restore can return your troubled PC to a healthy state.

Windows is capable of achieving this rolling back of time because it regularly creates snapshots of your computer's operating system called 'restore points'. System Restore records the system files and drivers on your PC at given times so that it knows how to return your PC to a state before it stopped working properly.

Automatic restore points

Windows automatically records an initial restore point when it is first launched. After that, it creates restore points at regular intervals. System restore points are also created whenever you install a new program or a Windows automatic update.

Creating your own restore point

If you are about to change your PC's settings or clear out some files and you're worried that you might destabilise your computer – for example, if you are installing a new scanner – create your own restore point before you start. That way you know that whatever you do, you will be able to return your system to its current working state. To do this, open the System Restore Wizard by clicking on the **Start** button and selecting **All Programs, Accessories, System Tools,** and then **System Restore**.

Put a dot next to 'Create a restore point' and click on **Next**. Give your new restore point a description that will remind you why you created it. For example, make a note of what you were about to install.

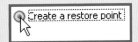

This appears along with the date and time you created the restore point in the description pane of the System Restore calender. When your new restore point is confirmed, click **OK** to finish.

Allocating disk space

Depending on how much you use your PC, System Restore tries to store about two weeks of past restore points. Because the snapshots take up a large amount of disk space, Windows deletes the oldest ones when it reaches its allowed limit. When Windows installs System Restore on your PC, it allocates about 12 per cent of your disk space for this storage. You can change the amount of disk space assigned to System Restore by clicking on the **Start** menu and selecting

Control Panel. Click on the **Performance and Maintenance** icon, then click **System** and select the **System Restore** tab. Determine how much disk space is allocated to the Restore function by adjusting the slider under 'Disk space usage'. Click on **Apply** and then **OK**.

If it all goes wrong

If you are not happy with your PC after restoring it to an earlier state, System Restore can undo its changes. If you've just completed a restoration, a third option appears when you open the System Restore Wizard. Select **Undo my last restoration** and click on **Next** to proceed. Alternatively, select **Restore my computer to an earlier time** again, and select a restore point prior to the last restoration you chose.

- ○ Restore my computer to an earlier time
- ○ Create a restore point
- ◉ Undo my last restoration

Close up
All the files in your My Documents folder and data files created between the roll back date and the present will be unchanged by System Restore; only system files, programs and drivers are removed.

Bright idea
If your PC develops a problem after you have installed a new program, try uninstalling the software in the normal way, using Add or Remove Programs (see page 74), before restoring your computer's system.

Reinstalling Windows

Occasionally you will encounter persistent problems with Windows. If you have tried all other remedies, the only solution is to reinstall. This restores the operating system files but leaves your work and programs unaffected. It is advisable to run Error-checking and Disk Defragmenter before reinstalling to help prevent problems occurring during installation.

SEE ALSO...
- *Maintain your hard disk* p 76
- *Windows won't start up* p 90
- *Program crashes* p 97

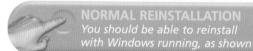

NORMAL REINSTALLATION
You should be able to reinstall with Windows running, as shown here. If you can't get Windows to start at all, see 'Starting without Windows' opposite.

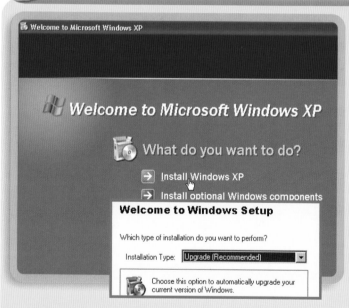

1 Put your Windows XP CD-ROM into the CD drive. If Setup does not start automatically, click on the **Start** button, **My Computer** and then on the CD-ROM drive icon (usually D:).

A window opens asking what you want to do. Click on the **Install Windows XP** link. At the next screen, select **Upgrade (Recommended)** from the 'Installation Type' list and click on **Next**.

2 Click on **Next** when the Windows Setup window opens. When you are asked, accept the License Agreement and click **Next**, then enter your product key or serial number from the Windows CD or manual cover. Click on **Next** and Setup will check that there is enough space to install Windows. All running programs will be closed so make sure you have already saved any work.

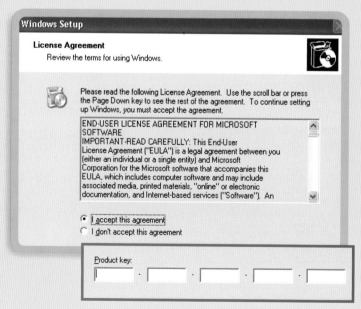

Starting without Windows

If Windows won't start up, you can put the Windows XP CD-ROM in the drive and try to start your PC using that – follow the instructions on the screen to repair or reinstall Windows. In case your PC is not able to start up from a disc in its CD drive, it is advisable to create special boot floppy disks. You can download the files you need from Microsoft's Web site. Go to www.microsoft.com, click on **Support**, select **Windows XP** from 'Select a Microsoft Product' and search for 'Windows XP Setup Boot Disks'. Follow the instructions under 'Obtaining Windows XP Setup Boot Disks'.

Watch out

Only reinstall Windows if System Restore (see page 100) did not resolve the problem. Always back up your data first (see page 78) and bear in mind that all programs and Windows updates will need to be reinstalled as well. If your PC came with a 'recovery disk', use that instead of reinstalling – follow the manufacturer's instructions.

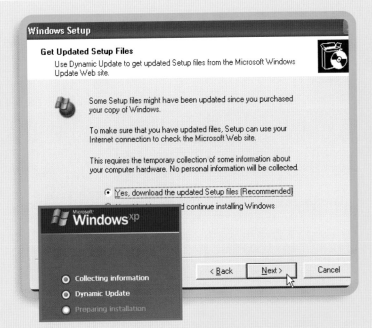

3 You will be asked whether you want to download updated Windows files from the Internet. Choose **Yes** if you have an Internet connection.

You can opt to do this after installation (see page 70). Then Windows will be reinstalled. As each stage is completed, a green dot appears next to its entry in the window.

4 During the final stage of installation, Windows sets up hardware devices and Desktop elements. These include items in the Control Panel and on the Start menu. Windows will restart your PC during this process. Click on **Finish** at the Thank you screen.

GLOSSARY

A

A: The floppy disk drive on a PC, also referred to as the 'A drive'. *See Floppy disk.*

Accessories Small programs, such as Calculator or Notepad, which are included with Windows.

Active window The window you are working in. To make a window active, click on it and it will 'jump' to the front. *See Window.*

Alt A key on the keyboard that activates a command when pressed in combination with other keys.

Application A piece of software designed to perform specific tasks. For example, Microsoft Word is a word-processing application that is used to create text documents. Also known as a program.

Archive To copy files that are no longer in use but need to be kept on a separate storage system, such as a Zip disk. *See Backup.*

Arrow keys *See Cursor keys.*

Attachment A file sent with an e-mail message.

Audio file A digital sound recording. Windows audio files usually have '.wav' or '.wma' as a suffix to the file name.

B

Backup A duplicate of a file or folder, made in case of loss or damage to the original data. Backups are usually made on removable disks, such as recordable CDs or Zip disks.

BIOS Basic Input/Output System. Instructions that control the communication between a PC and its hardware at a basic level.

Bit The smallest unit of computer storage, with a value of 1 or 0. 'Bit' is a contraction of 'binary digit'. All computers use the binary system to process data.

Bitmap An onscreen image made up of tiny dots or pixels. *See Pixels.*

Bits per second (bps) Units of measurement of the rate at which data can be transmitted.

Boot or **boot up** To switch on the PC, activating the BIOS.

Bug An error or fault in a program which can cause it to malfunction or crash, possibly leading to data loss.

Button An onscreen image that, when clicked on with the mouse, performs a function. For example, the 'OK' or 'Yes' buttons that confirm a proposed course of action.

Byte A unit of computer memory, made up of eight bits. One byte of memory stores the code for a single character, such as a letter of the alphabet.

C

C: Also called the 'C drive', this letter represents a PC's hard disk, on which all programs and documents are stored.

Cache A section of high-speed memory or disk space allocated to storing recently used data, thus increasing the speed at which that data can be accessed again.

CD-ROM Compact Disc–Read Only Memory. A storage device in the form of a CD, containing up to 700MB of data. Most software comes on CD-ROMs, which are inserted into the PC and usually accessed from the 'D drive'.

Cell A small rectangular area in a spreadsheet or database, into which text or figures can be entered. Click on a cell to make it active.

Chip A tiny circuit that processes or stores data. A processor chip carries out calculations and a memory chip stores data.

Click To press and release the left mouse button once. This is how menu and dialogue box options and toolbar buttons are selected.

Clip Art Graphic images supplied with Microsoft Office that can be inserted into documents.

Clipboard A virtual location where anything cut or copied is stored. The Windows Clipboard stores one piece of data at a time. A new cut or copied item will overwrite previous material on the Clipboard. Use the Paste command to insert a Clipboard item in a document.

Close A command on the File menu, which shuts down the active window or document, but leaves the program open. It serves the same function as clicking the black 'Close' button (not the red 'Exit' button).

CMOS Complementary Metal Oxide Semiconductor. A memory chip that stores your PC's BIOS configuration settings and the date and time.

Compression To reduce the size of files so they use less storage space and can be copied or downloaded more quickly.

Configuration The settings used to make sure your hardware and software run as you want them to.

Control key The two 'Ctrl' keys on the same row as the Space bar that can activate commands or shortcuts when pressed with other keys.

Control Panel A range of utility programs that enable you to control your Windows settings. For example, you can change the way your Desktop looks, add new hardware, or alter your PC's sound scheme.

Copy To make a duplicate of a file, folder, image, or section of a document.

CPU Central Processing Unit. The 'brain' of your PC, which carries out millions of arithmetic and control functions every second. Its power is defined by its speed in MegaHertz (MHz), or GigaHertz (GHz) – the number of times it makes a decision every second. For example, an 800MHz CPU carries out 800 million calculations per second.

Crash A program or operating system failure. Your PC has crashed if the screen 'freezes' and the keyboard or mouse commands do not work. You may need to restart the computer.

Cursor A marker, usually a flashing vertical line, indicating where any item typed, or inserted, will appear on the page.

Cursor keys The four arrow keys at the bottom right of the keyboard that move the insertion point or allow you to scroll through a window's contents.

Cut To remove selected files, folders, text or images to the Clipboard, where they are stored for later use.

D

Data Information processed or stored digitally on a computer.

Database A system for storing information so it can be easily accessed, organised, and sorted. Each entry is called a 'record', and each category in a record is called a 'field'.

Default Settings and preferences automatically adopted by your PC when no others have been specified by the user.

Delete To completely remove a selected file, folder, or image, or a piece of text from your document.

Desktop The background you see every time you use your PC, which can be personalised to suit your needs. Icons on the screen can represent office items, such as files, folders, and a recycle bin. The Taskbar and Start button allow you to access and organise your work.

Dialogue box A window that displays messages from the operating system or the program currently in use. This usually asks for confirmation of a proposed course of action or for information to be inputted by the user.

Dial-up connection The process of accessing an ISP's (Internet Service Provider) computer using a telephone line and a modem.

Digital image An image which is stored in binary format, so it can be viewed and changed on a PC.

Disk A device for storing digital information. A hard disk is made of a stack of rigid disks, known as 'platters'; a floppy disk uses just one flexible disk.

Disk Defragmenter A program that 'tidies' files on the hard disk. Occasionally Windows splits up a file when it is being saved so the file elements become fragmented. This makes retrieving the file slower. The Disk Defragmenter regroups related data.

Disk tools Programs that manage and maintain the data on the hard disk, making sure that it can be stored and retrieved efficiently.

Document A single piece of work created in a program, also referred to as a 'file'.

DOS Disk Operating System. Usually used to refer to the operating system for PCs before Windows.

Dots per inch (dpi) The number of dots per square inch that either make up an image on screen or that a printer has the capability to print. The more dots, the greater the detail and quality of the image.

Double-click To press and release the left mouse button twice in quick succession.

Download To copy files or programs from the Internet or from another computer to your own. You 'download' e-mail to read it.

Drag A mouse action used to select text, reshape objects, or to move an object or file. Click and keep the left button down. Then move the mouse as required and release.

Drive A device that holds a disk. A drive has a motor that spins the disk, and a head that reads and writes to it, in a similar way to the heads in a cassette deck.

Driver Software that communicates between Windows and a hardware device such as a printer or modem.

DVD Digital Versatile Disc or Digital Video Disc. A disk the same size as a CD but with a much larger storage capacity, up to 17GB. Because of this, DVDs can store whole movies with different languages, subtitles and extra footage.

E

E-mail Electronic mail. Messages that are sent from one computer to another using the Internet or any network.

Error message A small window on screen warning that a fault has occurred and possibly suggesting action to remedy it.

Expansion card Add-on hardware, which fits into a PC and expands its capabilities, such as a soundcard.

External hardware Additional computer equipment attached by cable to a PC, such as a printer.

F

Field An area of a database that contains a category of information, such as 'Name'.

File Any item that is stored on a computer, whether it is a program, a document, or an image.

File extension A three or four letter code assigned to the end of a file name when it is saved. This indicates the type of file so Windows knows which program to open it in. Also known as a suffix.

File format The way in which files created by different programs are saved. File formats are indicated by a code at the end of the file name. *See File extension.*

Floppy disk A portable storage device with 1.44MB capacity.

Folder A virtual storage location for files and programs.

Font A specific style and set of characters for a typeface, for example, Times New Roman.

Format (disks) To prepare a disk for storing and retrieving data for a specific operating system.

Format (documents) To alter a document's appearance, using style, typography, and layout options.

Freeware Programs which cost nothing and are often available to download from the Internet.

Function keys The 12 F keys running across the top of the keyboard, ranging from F1 to F12, which perform special tasks depending on the program.

G

.gif file Graphics Interchange Format. A file format for digital images used on Web sites.

Gigabyte (GB) A unit of memory capacity. One gigabyte consists of 1024 megabytes (MB).

H

Hard disk A computer's storage device containing the operating system, programs and all files. It is sometimes referred to as the 'C drive' or 'hard drive'.

Hardware The physical parts of a computer, including the system unit, monitor and keyboard.

Highlight To select text, images or cells by dragging the cursor over the item. See *Drag*.

I

Icon A graphical representation of a file or a function, for example, the Recycle Bin icon on the Desktop.

Import To bring text, images or files from one program into another.

Inkjet printer A printer that works by squirting tiny drops of ink onto the surface of the paper. Many home printers work in this way.

Install To copy a program's files onto the hard disk, and set it up ready for use. Programs are usually installed from CD-ROMs.

Internet A contraction of 'International Network'. It consists of millions of computers around the world, which are linked by phone and cable lines.

ISP Internet Service Provider. A company that provides a connection from your computer to the Internet.

J

Jaz disk A portable storage device capable of storing 2GB on one disk.

.jpeg Joint Photographics Experts Group. A file format that compresses images so they take up less space.

K

Keyboard shortcut A group of keys pressed simultaneously as a quick way of issuing a command.

Kilobit (Kb) A unit of data capacity normally used for data flow rates. A kilobit is 1024 bits.

Kilobyte (KB) A unit of data capacity. One kilobyte equals 1024 bytes. *See Gigabyte and Megabyte.*

L

Laptop A portable computer with a keyboard and flat screen.

Laser printer A type of printer that uses a laser to draw images electrostatically onto a drum and then transfers them to paper.

Log on To access a computer, file or Web site using a security procedure, such as a password.

M

Maximize To increase the size of a window to fill the entire screen.

Megabyte (MB) A unit of memory capacity. One megabyte equals 1024 kilobytes.

Memory Computer chips that store data. *See RAM and ROM.*

Menu bar A bar at the top of a window containing lists of options arranged by category. Click on a heading to see a drop-down menu of options.

Minimize To reduce a window to a button on the Taskbar.

Modem A device used to convert a computer's digital signals to and from analog signals that can be transmitted over phone lines. This enables your computer to connect to the Internet.

Monitor A piece of equipment that displays all your work on screen. This may work in a similar way to a TV screen or may be a flat monitor made up of thousands of tiny transistors.

Motherboard The circuit board on which the central processing unit (CPU), memory, and slots for expansion cards are mounted.

Mouse pointer

Mouse pointer A small arrow or cursor on screen controlled by the mouse. Pointers can be a pointing hand, a pen or a cross, depending on the program and the action.

Multimedia Computing that can combine audio, graphics, text and video.

My Computer A Windows folder. Open this to access your PC's hard disk, floppy disk and CD-ROM drive.

My Documents A special Windows folder designed to store files created by the user.

N

Network Interconnected computers (including other hardware) that share files and resources.

O

Open To bring a file, folder or program into use.

Operating system (OS) Software that controls the running of a computer. Microsoft Windows is the most popular OS for PCs.

Orientation The way that a page is meant to be viewed or printed, either 'Landscape' (longer horizontally) or 'Portrait' (longer vertically).

P

Page break The place where one page ends and another begins.

Parallel port A socket on the rear of a PC to which hardware, such as a printer, can be connected.

Paste To insert a file, folder, text or data that has been cut or copied.

PC-compatible

PC-compatible Software or hardware that works on a PC.

PCI slot A connector inside a PC into which you can fit circuit boards, such as a soundcard.

Peripheral A device, such as a scanner, that can be connected to a PC but is not central to its operation.

Pixels Individual dots on a screen. The number of pixels determines the level of detail and quality of display.

Plug-ins Hardware or software that adds extra functionality. Web sites often provide plug-ins for visitors to download, so that they can view all the content.

Port A socket at the back of a computer for connecting devices.

Print Preview The onscreen display of how a document will look when it is printed.

Processor The central processing unit (CPU) of a PC.

Program Software that interacts with the computer's hardware allowing the user to perform specific tasks.

Properties The attributes of a file or folder, such as its creation date, format and author's name.

R

RAM Random Access Memory. Memory chips used for temporary storage of information, such as the currently active file. As soon as the computer is switched off, this temporary information disappears.

Recycle Bin A Desktop feature used to store files ready for permanent deletion. To delete files in the Recycle Bin, right-click its icon and select Empty Recycle Bin.

Registry The Windows database of its configuration settings and installed programs.

Reset button A button on the system unit, usually below the power button, which allows users to restart their PC if it 'crashes'. It should only be used as a last resort.

Resolution The degree of detail on a screen or a printed document, measured in dots per inch (dpi). The higher the dpi, the better the detail.

Right-click To press and release the right mouse button once.

ROM Read Only Memory. Memory chips that are used for storing basic PC details.

Run command A Windows feature that allows you to launch a program by typing in its name.

S

Save To store or copy a document to a disk.

Save As Allows a file to be saved using a different name, drive or format, without affecting the original saved version.

Scanner A device which converts images and text to a digital format so they can be manipulated and reproduced by a computer. *See Digital image.*

Screensaver A picture or animation that appears on screen when the PC is left idle for a specified time.

Scroll To move through the contents of a window or menu vertically or horizontally.

Search A utility that searches a range of files for specified data, or which searches the hard disk for files or folders.

Search engines Databases on the Internet, which you can use to locate Web sites by typing in a key word or phrase.

Select To click on a file, folder, image, text, or other item, so it can be manipulated.

Serial port A socket at the rear of a computer previously used for modems and joysticks. *See Parallel Port.*

Shortcut An icon that provides quick access to a file, folder or program stored on the hard disk. A shortcut icon looks identical to the icon of the item to which it is linked but has a small overlaid arrow in the bottom left corner.

Software Programs that allow users to perform specific functions; Microsoft Excel and Microsoft Word are examples of software.

Software suite A collection of programs in a single package, for example, Microsoft Office.

Soundcard A device that lets users record, play and edit sound files. It fits into an expansion slot on the motherboard.

Sound file An audio file. To hear it, double-click on the file (you will need speakers and a soundcard).

Spreadsheet A document that stores and calculates data, used mainly for accounting and financial planning.

Start button The button to the left of the Taskbar, which accesses the 'Start' menu.

Status bar Strip at the bottom of a program window that displays information on the open document.

System files Windows' vital operating files.

System unit The PC box, containing the hard disk, the processor, memory, and sockets for peripheral devices, such as a printer.

T

Tab key A key (next to Q on the keyboard) used to tabulate text, to move between cells in spreadsheets, or to move from one database field to the next.

Taskbar A bar along the bottom of the screen that displays the Start button and buttons for all programs and documents currently open.

Template A document containing preset basic elements, which can be used as the basis for other documents.

Tile To reduce the size of a group of open windows, arranging them so they can all be seen at once.

Toolbar A bar or small window, which contains buttons and drop-down lists for issuing commands or accessing functions.

Typeface *See Font.*

U

Uninstall To remove programs from the PC's hard disk.

Upgrade To improve the performance or specification of a PC by adding new hardware, such as a higher capacity disk drive.

USB Universal Serial Bus. A hardware connector that allows users to plug in a number of devices, such as modems and scanners, to their PCs without having to restart.

Utilities Software that assists in housekeeping or troubleshooting computer functions.

V

View A menu category containing options that change the way a file is displayed on screen.

Virus A program designed to damage a computer system.

W

Window The self-contained viewing and working area of a folder or program. Several windows can be open at once on the Desktop.

Windows A popular operating system for PCs, which allows users to run many programs at once, opening files enclosed by frames called 'windows'.

Windows Explorer A program for viewing the contents of a PC's disks in a single window.

Wizard A program tool that guides users through a complex task.

Word processing Text-based operations carried out on the PC, such as letter writing.

World Wide Web The part of the Internet, composed of millions of linked Web pages, which can be viewed using Web browsing software, such as Internet Explorer.

Z

Zip disk A removable disk capable of storing up to 750MB of data.

Zip drive Drive for reading and writing Zip disks.

Zipped folder A special Windows folder that compresses files when they are dragged or copied to it. These folders are identifiable by the 'zipper' on the folder icon.

INDEX

Numbers shown in **bold** type represent the main references to the subject listed.

 **Reader's Digest**

For Reader's Digest

Editor
Caroline Boucher

Art Editor
Julie Bennett

Reader's Digest General Books

Editorial Director
Cortina Butler

Art Director
Nick Clark

Executive Editor
Julian Browne

Managing Editor
Alastair Holmes

Style Editor
Ron Pankhurst

This book was edited, designed and produced by

Planet Three Publishing Network
Northburgh House, 10 Northburgh Street,
London EC1V 0AT

Editor
Kevin Wiltshire

Sub Editor
Emily Kerry

Art Editor
Susan Gooding

Designer
Yuen Ching Lam

Authenticators
Tony Rilett, Pat Clark

Acknowledgments

We would like to thank the following individuals and organisations for their assistance in producing this book.

Picture Credits: Pages 57 and 58(bc) – 'Let Go', Avril Lavigne:- Album cover reproduced with the kind permission of Arista Records.

Photography: John Freeman

Software: Microsoft Press Office; Symantec

ISBN (10) 0 276 42832 3
    (13) 978 0 276 42832 6
Book code 400-187-03